North Staffordshire Hauliers

Ken Beresford Sr with Ken Jr in front of a Beresford Transport Foden S21 with 'Mickey Mouse' cab, 1960s. John Heath drove this for a while. *K Beresford Collection*

Ros Unwin

CHURNET VALLEY BOOKS
1 King Street, Leek, Staffordshire. ST13 5NW 01538 399033
www.leekbooks.co.uk
© Ros Unwin and Churnet Valley Books 2011
ISBN 9781904546801

In memory of Joe Unwin. Remembering also John Fowler and Bill Taylor

Front Cover:
A young Johnny Harding in front of KTU 434, the third ERF Belfields purchased from Bassets of Tipton. c1958.
J Harding Collection

Back Cover:
A Beresford 'tacho' from June 1979 when John Heath took a load of Johnson's tiles to Berlin. *John Heath Collection*

A Beresford ERF, XEH 283M leaving the ferry at Antwerp Docks en route to Luxembourg c 1975. The driver was Jack Kelly and the load was part of a Terex Dump Truck. This was one of five or six travelling in convoy. *John Heath*

THE OLD AND THE NEW

ABOVE: Jesse Shirley workers at their depot in Etruria c.1945 and Bedford lorry. Crawford Shirley is in the white coat on the right of the picture and his father Wilfred is at the front on the far right. *Courtesy Jesse Shirley, Etruria.*

BELOW: Brit European Belgium vehicle with trailer designed for carrying carpets. Photo outside Wembley Stadium
R Carman Collection

CONTENTS

ACKNOWLEDGEMENTS

Thanks to everyone who contributed and helped. Special thanks to Derek Hambleton, John Heathcote and Dave Unwin for pointing me in the right direction; to John Heath and Carl Johnson for their help with photographs; and to Dave Scarlett and Johnny Harding for putting the word about among the drivers. I'm sorry I didn't get to include everyone who wanted to be in - perhaps next time. If anyone has any Bartlam or Valance pictures I'd love to hear from you. Please forgive any errors, I've done my best.

An ERF with a Gardner 4LK engine at
Scholar Green Depot with garage staff
Ernest and Russell Pugh

A Foden with Foden two stroke engine at Scholar Green Depot 1960s

A 1950 Foden, 2 stroke engine with Dyson Air
Ride trailer. The first venture into articulated
vehicles. Taken at Scholar Green Depot

W CARMAN & SON: Ron Carman

My father, William Carman, was born in 1890. He came from a farming family; his father had a farm in Scholar Green. Father was in the Lancashire Fusiliers during the First World War but prior to that was in service to the family that owned Coates Cottons in Scotland. After the war he went into service again at Peckforten Castle.

At some stage he decided he was going to start up in transport. In those days he was using horses and carts to transport stone from Mow Cop Station which was used to make roads. He was also dealing in hay and straw. He'd buy the straw and transport it to the pot banks where it would be used for packing pottery in crates.

Eventually, he went on to purchase ex-army vehicles - makes unheard of nowadays such as the Straker Squire and the Vulcan. However his first vehicle was a Royal Air Force-type Leyland with which he started to transport pottery all over the country. He would talk about driving a vehicle on solid tyres with no side curtains to the cab. There were no kerbs at the side of the road and he had a pair of oil lamps as a means of lighting. He was travelling to London, Glasgow etc. A journey to London would be a day's work.

Later, he became involved in the collection of milk from Cheshire farmers, delivering to the Manchester dairies. In order to obtain the work he would go to the individual farmers and offer to take them to Manchester to introduce them to the various dairymen. If a negotiation by the dairyman to buy the milk was accomplished then he would ensure that he'd do the transport. He was paid by the farmers.

He told me stories, among many others, of taking milk from Mrs Foden's farm. Mrs Foden was part of the Foden family who were involved in the production of steam wagons. This would be in the early 1930s and I know at this time he had Vulcan vehicles.

By the late 1930s he had a couple of vehicles - a Bedford, and an Albion which was pre-Clydesdale. I left school in 1940 at 16 and the Milk Marketing Board was now directing the milk to individual dairies in different parts of the country. Father was contracted to them. By this time I was working in the business as a second-mate to Arthur Lockett. Arthur and I loaded milk churns at the various farms by standing each side of the churns, right hand in my case, under the bottom rim, left hand on the handle at the top and lifting 15 gallons of milk (300lbs plus) onto the vehicle. Having loaded up we went on our journey to Heald's Dairies in Didsbury and Allied Dairies in Manchester.

We would collect the churns from the farms at 8.00am at the latest. We unloaded at the dairy and put the empty churns back on the vehicle. From Manchester we then went to various dairies such as at Whitchurch,

Albion KO127 (petrol) used for collection of milk in churns from Cheshire farms to the Co-op Dairy Manchester, 1940s. Norman Sherratt. All Carman vehicles had a film star's name written above the cab at this time.

Ellesmere, Uttoxeter and Corwen in North Wales. We'd collect a load of churns full of milk and take it to Manchester. We'd return home having done 12-14 hours work.

In 1942 I joined the army and father continued to develop the business with bulk tankers. When I say bulk tankers I don't mean the tankers with their fancy pumping equipment that are used these days to collect milk from the farms - more like the ones used for the transport of chemicals and petrol etc. Father's vehicles were operating under the direction of the Ministry of Food from, say, United Dairies and taking the milk into what was called the 'liquid market'. Father's first tanker was a four wheel Foden with an LK Gardner engine capable of carrying 1200-1500 gallons of milk.

I came out of the army in 1945/46 and went back in to the business working in the workshop, bodyshop and paintshop. By this time we had acquired two or three tankers - their capacity was now 1500 gallons and they were fixed to the chassis of ERFs. I remember we acquired an ex-military Foden six wheeler with a Gardner 6LW engine from Beech's Garage and converted it into an eight wheeler fixed with a bulk milk tanker. On the cab door of that vehicle was written W Carman, The Bungalow, Scholar Green. My father wouldn't display anything else. He made it clear he was the sole owner of the business with no other party involved. He wouldn't hear of it if one talked about being a Limited Liability company.

Then nationalization came along but because of the nature of the business - bulk transport from dairy to dairy - British Road Services never acquired our company as it wasn't suited to their type of operation. We went on to purchase a milk churn collection and delivery business owned by a Mrs Riley and her daughter based at Allostock in the Knutsford area. This was attractive because its location was within the fifty mile freedom limit - they could get from Allostock to Manchester and Liverpool without a permit which we couldn't do from Scholar Green.

Having purchased this business, three other operators who were free from the government restrictions, were invited to participate. One was Leslie Kitchen based not far from Peckforten Castle who delivered milk churns to Liverpool. Another was Harry Swain from Macclesfield who delivered to Manchester (still going today under F Swain & Sons Limited) and Les

A Foden with a 5LW Gardner engine used for milk transport from dairy to dairy.

Boughey based at Nantwich who transported to Liverpool. The company was called Riley's Transport Allostock Limited. Within a short space of time Riley's grew and became engaged in the transport of tinned goods from Liverpool to the Potteries.

By the time of de-nationalization the shares owned by the other three parties had been acquired by W Carman and acquisitions of vehicles and licences from BRS were made. The fleet grew rapidly. The trucks acquired from BRS traded under the name of W Carman and Son. The reason for this was that in the event of the Labour party coming into power again with similar thoughts on nationalization these vehicles, which were now beginning to engage in transport of goods all over the country, would be separate from the original base organisation (W Carman) and not be subject to nationalization. That was the thinking.

In the 1950s I became involved in the running of the business. In the 1930s and 40s my father had enjoyed an excellent relationship with the manager of the Nestle Dairy at Middlewich who by this time was Managing Director of Nestle UK in Croydon. This put me in a good position to approach them to carry their goods. Very quickly we were moving goods for all the Nestle companies - Tutbury, Ashbourne, Carlisle, Aylesbury, Chippenham, Staverton and Hayes. We also opened a depot at Trowbridge in Wiltshire at the invitation of Nestle who wanted to dispose of the services of BRS.

During the 1950s, if I wanted to have a licence other than purchased from BRS, I had to go to the North Western Traffic Area Licensing Authority and produce figures to prove a customer needed our transport. I also had to engage the services of a witness for the company concerned. If successful, the Authority would give you an 'A' or 'B' licence to operate another vehicle - preferably an 'A'. We were subject to objection by British Rail and, of course, other transport operators who would appear in court to say that I didn't need a particular licence. I remember that Arthur and Hilda Davey always came along to my application hearings. In the late 1950s the fleet was about sixty or seventy vehicles strong.

In about 1942 my father had bought a smallholding in Scholar Green and, by degrees, it was converted into offices, a workshop, body shop, paint shop and vehicle washing area. The site was about 3-4 acres with warehousing for storage. We stored tinned milk and cream for Nestle, tinned beans etc for Heinz, tin cans for Metal Box as well as providing heated warehousing for sugar. The vehicle fleet consisted of mainly ERFs but also Foden and Albions. We had the odd Leyland and Scammell but these were vehicles that came from BRS.

By the early 1960s we'd acquired J Sullivan, a company based in London, which was involved in transporting Nestle goods to London docks for export. In 1962 Colonel Bustard and his two sons, all of whom I came to know, started cross-channel ferry services from Tilbury to the old Rotterdam docks and also to Antwerp. At about this time we undertook our first cross-channel contract for Johnson's Polish taking 80 tons of polish to a place near Dusseldorf. Discussions with the sons of Colonel Bustard resulted in a bond with them and they gave us excellent sea ferry rates.

With the commencement of the cross-channel ferry operations we had to equip ourselves with some trailers capable of being sealed to carry the order. I went along to Boalloy at Congleton. I sat down with Gerald Broadbent and we devised a means of converting flat trailers to the type known as TIR - Transport International Routier. These were trailers capable of being sealed so HM Customs could ensure that export duty had been paid on departure from the UK and no interference with the load could occur until received at the delivery point.

In order to send a trailer without a tractor unit we had to have an associate who would undertake to move the trailers from the port of import to their destination. It would be the duty of this haulier to find return loads from the continent. This was necessary because the rates we quoted didn't include the cost of shipping the trailers back empty. We found such a company, Wetram, owned by Johnny Van der Ven and Johnny Figay, and the arrangement worked well.

It was obvious to me that there was considerable potential for growth and I therefore engaged a man named Keith Paynter who had previously been employed by Continental Ferry

Trailers Limited, part of the Transport Development Group. He had a great deal of knowledge of this type of operation and set about developing the business. Very quickly we were shipping trailers out of the UK at a rate of 10 a day. By this time we were not only engaged in the shipment of dry goods but also bulk liquids and temperature controlled loads. When the agreement with Wetram came to an end I formed Brit European Netherlands. This would be in the 1970s.

It became obvious that the Belgian port of entry, Antwerp, was preferable to the port of Rotterdam unless, of course, you were shipping to northern Germany. However, Antwerp was being replaced by the coastal port of Zeebruge which didn't have the problems that Antwerp had of having to go through locks. The port of exit from the UK had moved from Tilbury to Felixstowe, again coastal. I decided, therefore, to form Brit European Belgium and Eurolines Belgium. The interest in Belgium proved to be correct and we now have a depot of about 5 acres within the port of Zeebruge with warehousing. We operate 24 hours a day, 7 days a week and have a fleet of 100 vehicles involved solely in the distribution of Belgian carpets to the UK.

In the 1970s JCB were developing exports to Europe so I went along to see Mr Joe Bamford and in due course secured business. This relationship with Bamfords has led to the present situation where we are the biggest supplier of transport to JCB with contracts to undertake the whole of the UK distribution to depots and agents. We do the export movements to the UK ports for deep sea shipments to such countries as America, India and other countries in which JCB have established facilities. Alongside this we do cross channel shipments to Germany, Belgium and Eastern bloc countries with staff on site at various UK JCB factories to load our vehicles and other transport suppliers' vehicles.

Since the 1990s development at Brit European has been in the shipment of commercial vehicles on our specialized trailers. MAN Germany supplies the British Forces with heavy military vehicles and we transport these from Germany to the UK. We also transport cars for Honda, Audi and Porsche and commercial vehicles for Mercedes, Renault, Scania and Iveco coming in to the UK. We have upwards of 40 vehicles engaged in car transport and approximately 60 vehicles for JCB and MOD movements.

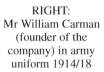

LEFT:
Mr Ron Carman in
army uniform
1942/46

RIGHT:
Mr William Carman
(founder of the
company) in army
uniform 1914/18

ABOVE:
Opening of the Euro Tunnel,
Folkestone to Calais. Brit European
vehicles were among the first to use
this new crossing.

Mr Ron Carman with son Rod in the 1980s.

Shipment of trailers to
Rotterdam NL at
Felixstowe Docks. At this
time Brit European
Transport had its own
office in Felixstowe
Docks. c.1994

Car-carrying vehicle able to carry 11 cars. 2008.

All photos R Carman Collection

Foden with TIR trailer (Transport International Routiers) for JCB Exports. 1970s.

H TIDESWELL & SONS LIMITED

Eric Tideswell

Herman Tideswell, my father, was born at Cauldon Low in 1905. Dad set up in business in 1924 with a horse and cart, repairing roads using sand and gravel that he hauled from Highshut Quarry. He bought his first vehicle, a Leyland, in about 1928.

Herman Tideswell, front, c 1928 with Leyland vehicle.

By this time he was doing work for Wiltshire United Dairies (later United Dairies and eventually Unigate) at Uttoxeter. He was fetching sugar from Liverpool to go into sweetened milk. The loads then would be 5 or 6 tons of 2 cwt bags which were, of course, loaded by hand. In 1931 he bought a new AEC.

When he and my mother got married they lived at Woodhouse for a while but moved to Glebe House, Kingsley, where we are now, in 1936. They had six children: Joan, Roy, Me, Barbara, Winifred and Trevor.

At the time of nationalization all the vehicles were on contract licences to United Dairies. At about this time Dad bought Parkfields Farm in Cherry Lane, Cheadle, which Uncle Jack, known as the Colonel, ran. At its height in the 1960s H Tideswell & Sons had 25 vehicles. Mum did all the admin work. She'd be making phone calls from 9.30 until 11.00 in the mornings then have lunch and be back on the phone again from 2.00 until 4.00 in the afternoons. She'd be arranging things; wagons would be coming in and the loads would be swapped. She was on the ball. The vehicles were all rigids at this time - we had our first artic in June 1967. What is now the kitchen was a store for nuts and bolts but later became the office.

Roy and I were the mechanics. I put an eight cylinder Gardner engine in an F88 Volvo once. Anyway, some men who had heard about it came over and asked if they could have a look. I said 'Yes, it comes in at about five-o-clock.' They couldn't believe we'd got it working. We had to break it up when the time came to sell it.

Dad always wore a bow tie with Double Diamond written on it. They used to say that when a driver rang in and said there was a noise on the engine he would tell them to fetch it to the phone so he could listen to it! Dad also had a couple of taxis at one time - Ernie 'Pop' Ainsworth used to drive for him. When we became a limited company, Harold Barlow, who used to be a driver for us, managed the business with Dad. Trevor did the office work. Then we had a chap named Simon Parr. We also had a part-time secretary who used to do the wages and booking in and out etc. Simon and Trevor used to organise all the work up until 2008.

Pauline Tideswell

When I married Eric it was intended that we'd live on the farm. However, Herman sold it so we came to live here at Glebe House. Living here at one time with Mum and Dad were: Eric and I; Barbara and her first husband and their daughter, Charlotte; Winifred and Desmond and their son, Carl.

I've known Eric since I was twelve. I remember once he picked me up from the school gates when he was going to a breakdown at the dairy in Morton in Marsh. I'd be fifteen at the time. We hadn't got time to tell my mum so I just went with him. When we got down there we'd got nothing to eat and no money between us so we pinched a pint of milk each from the dairy. When I got home at about 6.30 the next morning, my mum had this policeman sitting there and I had to explain everything to him because I was actually a minor.

'JJ' was one of the first Tideswell AECs. This was rebuilt by Eric in the 1960s.

When we were courting we never went to discos or anything like that - we were always working. There's a picture of one of Herman's first AECs which Eric rebuilt. I helped him with it; that's the sort of thing we did when we were courting.

I'll never forget what Herman said when I told him we were getting married: 'Aye, when?' I told him October 20th. He said 'You're not.' I looked at him and he said 'If that's a Saturday, you can't. These wagons have to be serviced on a Saturday. Make it a Sunday, Monday or a Tuesday. A Tuesday would be better than a Monday.' So I got married at a quarter past twelve at St Werburgh's Church in Kingsley on a Tuesday. We both went back to work the next day because I worked for Herman's sister as a hairdresser and Eric worked for his dad.

Raymond Hine

I started to work for Tideswells in the early 1960s, working in the garage mainly but doing the occasional driving job. All the lorries were on contract to the dairies; there'd always be a load of butter in the yard. You'd go down to Uttoxeter and handball 15 tons of butter off and then perhaps go over to Whitchurch. Next day you'd nip down to Trowbridge in Wiltshire and load Unigate stuff, jam and all that, and then you'd be off to East Kilbride in Scotland. This would be in an eight wheel van and this jam would be in 5

Raymond Hine at the wheel of a Volvo. Ken Brindley always did the signwriting for Tideswell vehicles. *Raymond Hine Collection.*

gallon galvanised tins.Then it would be across to Edinburgh and load fondant back to Trowbridge. Fondant is like marshmallow; ever so strange but Unigate did a lot of products then.

Another job that had to be done at weekends was greasing the lorries. That was a fair job. There were 25 eight wheelers there then. We were just starting on artics. You'd do half the vehicles one week and the other half the next. It would take all day Saturday, out in the freezing cold.

In the 1970s I got hijacked in Scotland. I was parked in Pollockshields, near Glasgow with a load of butter from Uttoxeter. I went up on the Sunday and I parked up on this industrial estate. Of course, there were no pubs open on Sunday in Scotland, only hotels so I walked down to this hotel and had a drink. It was a summer's evening. I came back to the lorry and stripped off ready to sleep in the cab overnight. I'd only got my underpants on. Anyway, the street light went out and I thought it was odd. Then there's a knock on the door *'Give us your keys'*. And there are these guys with bricks in their hands. What do you do? I said *'Wait a minute'* and one of them ripped the curtain out of the cab. I said *'You can have the keys and the lorry.'* Anyway, they got in the back of the van and took some butter off. What they wanted really was beef.

So then they broke into this cold store and set the alarms off and that's when the police arrived. I was shaking like a leaf. The police said *'You don't want to be parking here; it's dangerous with these gangs'*. A bit late! Any road, they locked me up in the police station for the night because I refused to stay in the lorry. Then I had a good breakfast the next morning and they took me back to the lorry. I rang Tideswells because I'd got no keys. So I had to cut the Waso lock off the steering and start it up with a screw driver. A Scottish lad said *'If you can get the unit from under your trailer, I'll back it on for you and tip it'*. So I'm standing there with a hack saw blade sawing through the four bolts that hold the waso on the steering lock.

Anyway, when I came back home and go into Tideswell's yard they look at the lorry *'Oh, yes, we can fix this'*. So I go into the traffic office and the bloke says *'You know when you fall off a horse they say the best thing is to get back on again?'*. I said *'Yes'*. *'Well, we've got another load from Uttoxeter to the same place'*. So that's what I did. Anyway, I never told my wife anything about the hijacking but I got back at the weekend and it's headline news in the *Cheadle and Tean Times* *'Cheadle lorry driver in hijack drama'*. All about me, where I lived and everything!

There are some funny things I remember about Herman Tideswell. When the Michelin rep first came with the radial tyres Herman said *'They're no good, they're flat'*. The man said *'No, these are the new tyres'*. So Herman says to the lad who worked in the garage, *'Maurice, wheel the barrow round the yard'*. So he gets the barrow and he puts an old lorry wheel in it and wheels it around. He comes back. *'Now, let the tyre down a bit'*. So he does this and when he tries to push it the wheelbarrow is all over the place. So Mr Tideswell politely told the Michelin guy to go away! This rep told this story for years after that.

Herman was a great bloke. He'd lend you money. He loved it if you'd got a mortgage because he knew you'd work then. But wherever you went you'd only got to mention the Tideswell name and you could get anything done. I remember I broke down in Wincanton one night and tried to get someone out to me. They said *'Oh, no, we can't come out at this time of night'*. When I said I was a driver for Tideswells they said *'Oh, won't be long, mate'*. They'd leave other jobs to come and help.

There weren't any heaters in the wagons in those days - travelling to Scotland we would be absolutely frozen. You'd have old sack bags around your knees. You'd go out and all the ropes and sheets would be rock hard and your fingers were all cracked. But you got on with it. You had to. I can remember sitting in the canteen one winter's day when the snow was bad and one of the lads came in from Scotland and Eric says to him *'What's it like coming in today, mate?'* He said *'Shap was blocked when I came through!'*

I can remember Colin Clacher - he was a hero. He had an eight wheeler van with a side door. He always came in with something - he could get anything. I don't know how he did it. We still don't know how he did his job because he used to park on the Master Potter at Cheadle and his lorry would be there at half past seven in a morning and he'd got to go to East Kilbride and back. And you'd wonder how the hell he has done it. He was off once and this other chap took his eight wheeler. Colin was always complaining about it boiling up. Herman said to this chap, *'See what you think of it'*. He came back and said *'I'll tell you what's up with that wagon, Mr Tideswell, it's too fast for the water system'*. It couldn't keep itself cool.

Another chap started one day and was sent to Crewe. Anyway, he rang up the office and said *'I don't want to bother you, Mr Tideswell, but there's no oil pressure on this lorry'*. *'Was there any when you left the yard?'* said Herman. *'Yes'* replied the driver. *'Well, you were very lucky, then'*.

I still see Dave Barber from Cheadle who worked there when I did. There was also a lad from Biddulph Moor, Rod Brocklehurst. He was the tidiest sheet and roper anyone could ever wish for. He used to sheet a load and rope it and there wouldn't be a rope out of place - everything was perfectly in line.

We'd go up to Grimsby and pick Lurpak butter up on a flatbed lorry on a summer's day. We used to rope and sheet and if it was really warm we had to re-do it half way down to Uttoxeter because the bottom boxes would be collapsed, melted. We used to pick 45 gallon drums of condensed milk up from Uttoxeter. We had to stand them up ourselves, about 6.5 cwt. We'd take them to all the toffee factories: Barker and Dobson's, Kendal Mint Cake, Needlers of Hull. Colin Clacher backed into the yard at Barker and Dobson's one day and said to this chap *'What do you have to do to get any sweets round here, mate?'* This man says *'You can only have them if they're damaged'*. So the next time Colin goes he backs into all this stuff and the man says *'Bloody hell, mate, you've damaged 'em'*. Colin says *'Oh, I can have some now, can I?'*

After Herman died they decided to have a union at Tideswells and Colin was going to be shop steward. Anyway, there was a lot of trouble about it and they went on strike for seven weeks. It made headline news in the papers - *'We'll sell firm'*.

I was a bearer at his funeral along with Colin. I remember it absolutely poured with rain that day and Colin said *'It won't be the first time I've got drenched for Herman'*. Herman was a good bloke, well-liked.

AEC Mammoth Major Mk III 6-wheel milk tanker which used to be driven by Stan Walford. Eric still has it - in a state! *Aubrey Delderfield*

The Strike which hit the national newspapers. It didn't take long for the papers to come up with headlines for this dispute 'The Brothers' - a reference to the popular TV series at the time. The strikers are L-R: Stan Clarke, Roger Wright, Arthur Garrett, Johnny Edwards, Geoff Stevens, Les Wilshaw and Colin Clacher.

LEFT:
The Tideswell men: Roy, Eric, Trevor and Herman.

A 1950 Mk III - this was driven by Colin Clacher in the early 1960s.
Peter Davies

Pauline and Eric Tideswell 2005.

Tideswell Collection

Herman and Doris Tideswell

This was an ex-Trumans of Derby. The driver is Roy Tideswell. 1970s. *Carl Johnson Collection*

Raymond Hine
standing beside an
ERF.
*Raymond Hine
Collection*

**Tideswells changed to ERFs in 1972.
The Atki in the line-up in the photo above
was driven by Pete Smith.**
Carl Johnson Collection

BILL AND JOHN WASS: W & J WASS LIMITED

Tony Wass

My father, Bill Wass, was born in Fenton in 1910. He was one of sixteen children. His father, my grandfather, started to work as a carter for his brother, Harry, when he left the army after WW1. He lived and worked at Edgefields Farm at the back of Mossfield Colliery.

Obviously, in those days the carting was done by horses. Dad left school at 13 even though the school-leaving age at that time was 14. He said he needed to help his father support the family and refused to go back. He worked for his Uncle Harry on and off for a few years, carting coal and pottery. At around the time that Uncle Harry died and Dad thought *'If I'm working this hard for someone else, I can do it for myself'* and decided to set up on his own.

A very young Bill Wass (born 1910) standing first right.

This was in 1937. The only problem was he didn't have a horse. So he went to Ernie Hughes, a local horse dealer, who agreed to lend or rent him one. Then he managed to borrow some money to buy a harness and, using his father's old cart, started working for himself. The first job he took was one of Uncle Harry's old contracts at the Co-op factory in Longton. After that he took on another factory and then another. He kept buying horses and by about 1940 he had six or seven men driving different horses for factories in Longton and Fenton.

He also rented some stables from the coal board. In those days horses were often stabled at the factory where they worked and dad would buy horses in order to get work. He bought Cartwright and Edwards' five horses which were stabled there and another three from a carter in Longton named Collingwood who used to do Shaw and Collier's work.

I was born in 1941 at Edgefields and we ran about 15 horses from there after the war. I can remember my dad saying one morning that he'd sent 49 horses out to work that day. In 1946 my Uncle Jack, dad's brother, who was an engineer at Radway Green during the war, wanted to come into the business. At first they thought about getting some more horses but dad decided that lorries were the future and they went to Len Shortland Motors in Longton and bought a Dodge wagon. I can still remember the registration no.- LVT 38 - a Surrey Dodge. Dad had to drive it because Uncle Jack couldn't drive lorries at that time. Later they bought another two from him: LVT 42 and LVT43. By 1948 they had ten lorries and as they kept buying lorries they gradually phased out the horses.

Len Shortland was very helpful in the early years because he would let them borrow wagons - he would say *'Go and work them for a month and we'll sort out payments later'*. This really helped to get work. Len Hurst at Longton Transport did the same and Norman Beech was a great help when we started long-distance work. The first artic we had was a Dodge in 1961 followed by an ERF.

I can remember a driver didn't turn up one day and I said *'I can handle it'*. After I'd proved I could do it they would hardly let me get out of the cab! That was in 1962, I was just 21. They expected you to work hard. Sometimes I'd say to my dad *'What time are we finishing'* and he'd say *'When it goes dark'*. I never had to pass a test as far as artics were concerned - I automatically got a licence because I'd been doing it for so long. It was the same with the CPC Transport Managers' Licence and the International Transport Licence.

We started doing continental work in 1991/1992 taking special process clay over from Stoke (English China Clay) to Paris and bringing yellow clay back for a company in Trentham who used it to manufacture adhesives. It was good work as they needed 100-200 tons a week. We started going to Spain and Germany as well but the rates weren't very good and when the Trentham work dried up we called it a day with the continental work.

We did a lot of coal work. When I first started driving, after I'd done a stint in the garage to learn the mechanical side of things, I was on six and eight wheel tippers transporting coal to power stations. I remember doing the Ironbridge Power Station run for about 18 months. We moved coal from most of the local collieries: Mossfield, Florence, Glebe and Silverdale with Weston Wharf being our main one. We took coal to the main hospitals, Queen Elizabeth's in Birmingham was one and we did police depots and prisons. We went anywhere that had coal-fired boilers.

It was the same for the bottle ovens and kilns on the pot banks. In the mornings we'd take about five 10 ton loads in tipping lorries. At lunch time we'd come back to the depot and, if we were lucky, have something to eat. Then we'd wash the wagon and go on to clay in the afternoon. If you came in in the afternoon at about 4.30 or 5.00 you couldn't expect to knock off, you'd be sent on another job. Sometimes it would be nine or ten at night by the time you'd finished.

The clay came up from Cornwall and Devon on 12 ton trucks to the sidings at Longton, Tunstall, Longport, Burslem, Spath etc. We'd collect from there and take 24 tons (two trucks) to pot banks like Carlyles, Menzies, Ridgeways, Doultons and Wedgwoods. That was until English China Clays built a depot in Stoke and started bringing it in 100 ton loads on Tiger Trains. That's when we started using tankers.

Another thing you had to do when you'd done your coal and clay was 'scrap' from the pot banks. They had what they called the Swath Hole which was a big building full of pottery waste. We used to back the lorries in and chuck it on. If there were saggers you would put them to one side and load them separately. Daisy Bank Works used to crush them and the crushed material would go into making new saggers and sagger bottoms, that sort of thing. They used to give the drivers a shilling a ton. Then it went up to five shillings and then 10 shillings. It was how the drivers would make a bit of money on the side.

We used to do quite a lot of work for Campbell Tiles in Stoke and a bit for H & R Johnson (although Beresfords did most of their work) as well as Allied at Adderley Green. We would take tiles around the country to building contractors doing public buildings, hospitals etc. They were all transported in boxes. It was in the days before forklifts so when you got to where you were going you'd often have to unload it yourself by hand. Mintons did specialist tiles and I can remember taking five loads of their tiles down to Southampton Docks destined for The White House in Washington. When I was 21 I went to America with my cousin and two friends for eight weeks and I made a point of going on The White House tour and, sure enough, there were the Minton tiles I'd taken down to Southampton.

There were a lot of factories in the Potteries making fireplace tiles. We did work for Staffordshire Fireplaces and Abbey Tiles in Burslem. I once took two loads of fireplaces to the Outer Hebrides on a four wheeler. I had to catch about three barges. The first one was at Faze Lane, Glasgow. McBrides were the people who ran them from there. Then I took a McBrain's barge to another island. I did about three to get to the Orkneys. I think that was in 1966, the year I got married. I was away for about three weeks; loading and getting back and reloading in Glasgow.

You never knew when you were coming home because if you couldn't get a load home you'd have to go to somewhere else. We had a depot in Glasgow and sometimes I'd be told *'You'd better go into there and do a couple of days sorting out'*. There would always be stuff in the warehouse that our guys had dropped off because they couldn't deliver or were too late or something. Anyway, I'd have to do those loads taking them to Edinburgh or Fife or somewhere like that.

My dad would still drive a wagon if a driver didn't turn up; he would do this until he was nearly seventy. Uncle Jack was the same. Uncle Jack had a bit of a temper. He wouldn't put up with drivers who did something wrong. I remember him in the wharf one day in the days when we still had horses. My dad was in the cart chucking this coal over and a chap was saying *'We want this here'* and *'you've had enough'* and moved the horse out. My dad didn't notice but Uncle Jack was standing on the other side and said 'You put that horse back in there or else'. The man said something else and Uncle Jack hit him so hard that one of his eyes was hanging out on his cheek. I was only young. I was terrified. They took the man to Longton Cottage

Early 1940s. Mrs Plant (wife of Richard, the owner of RH & S L Plant) outside the factory making a presentation to Gordon Humphries on his retirement. Front L-R: Graham Bromley, Cyril Shipley, Gordon Humphreys, Mrs Plant, Bill's horse, 'Happy' Jones and Bill Wass. The man with the glasses immediately behind Gordon is Richard Plant, the owner. Bill's mum worked on the factory and is standing at the back on the left.

Hospital but nothing ever came of it. Uncle Jack wasn't tall but was stout and as strong as an ox. My dad didn't agree with a lot of things he did as he upset such a lot of people. My dad used to say to him *'Leave it to me to sort out'*.

We were the first people in the area to start using skips in the 1960s. We first saw one in Wigan and my dad said *'They're handy things'*. We got talking to the man who owned it and bought the lorry there and then. We soon bought another ten skips from him and eventually had 300 skips and five skip lorries.

Eventually, we got rid of a lot of the long-distance work and kept the local stuff. I took over part of the business in 1999 but I finished completely in 2007.

My father was one of the founders of the Road Haulage Association in Stoke; he was at various times on the committee and chairman. Throughout his life and career he did a lot for the local area. He never retired. He was a boy from a large family with no education who built up a fleet of over a hundred lorries. He was a councillor for Stoke on Trent for thirty years, a Justice of the Peace for 40 years and an Honorary Justice as well. He was Lord Mayor of Stoke on Trent in 1978 when he was in his seventies and did an enormous amount of engagements; he never turned anything down. My father and his brother were genuine, hard working men. They helped a lot of people. They never liked to let anyone down.

Although dad was very successful with his wagons he was a horse man at heart and we always kept show horses. I remember in the 1950s we had dapple greys and they were sent for to pull the coach for the Duke and Duchess of Devonshire at the Coronation. We actually took four down to London. A friend of ours, Reg Brewes, was also supplying two but one went lame and they wanted one of ours. Unfortunately, our horse didn't match his so they ended up using all four of ours; the other two horses pulled the carriage of the Duke and Duchess of Rutland.

I've continued with the horse tradition and am a director of the Shire Horse Society having recently received my Fifty Year medal from them. I'm also a show judge. I've always loved horses and everything I know about them I learned from my father.

The only picture we can find of Shortlands is at a show c 1960. *Sandra Hallam.*

C.1969 when George Bowers, the last of the horse men, retired.
L-R: Bill Wass, ?, Bill Clewlow, Horace Plant, ?, Alan Irvin,
Len Bowers, Graham Bowers, George Bowers, Alan Johnson,
Graham Cooke, Maurice Didd.

RIGHT: Bill Wass (left) with brother, John.

A Morris commercial used for
transporting special cartons to
stores in London and Scotland
1966/67.

A Guy carrying the load for the QE2 from North Staffs Potteries at Cobridge. Tony is driving with Bill passenger.

All photos Tony Wass Collection

Bill Wass during his time as Lord Mayor of Stoke on Trent with his wife, Florence, 1978/79.

ADAMS BUTTER: Alan Smith, Trevor Sales, John Lancaster and Les Bailey
Alan Smith

Fred Adams Snr started the butter business around 1915 on his father's farm. He had two sons; Fred Jnr took over after him as managing director and his other son, John, became company chairman. He also had a daughter Christine. The Adams family provided a great deal of employment in Leek and I personally found them to be fair employers and to this day am still in contact with them.

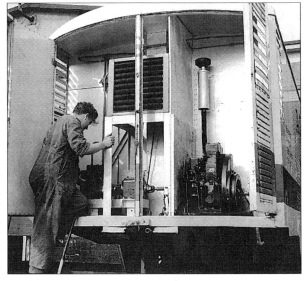

Picture showing fridge plant. 1960s.

I started at Adams in 1954 as an electrical engineer, later becoming development engineer after the retirement of Don Rider. I worked there for nearly 50 years, as far as I know the longest service in the company. In 1964 Adams employed about 430 people and, after outgrowing the Springfield Road site, moved the transport department to a new, purpose built, state of the art transport complex at Barnfields.

Adams Butter were blenders and packers and did not make butter although it is believed that Fred Adams did start by making it in a small way around 1929.

They'd fetch the butter from the docks - London, Hull, Grimsby and Liverpool - every day. Drivers would go out in the morning, do their deliveries and bring in a return load from one of the docks, often stopping overnight. The vehicles often worked night and day and, in the early days with the old Bedfords, they would be overloaded and would have to be towed up Upper Hulme, a steep hill on the outskirts of Leek.

At the business's peak they ran about 200 vehicles. There was a team of about 30 people working three shifts to keep the trucks on the road. I became involved in the transport side of things when they needed to refrigerate the trailers. Don Rider and I started to build these fridge units using Lister diesel engines, refrigeration compressors, gear boxes, electric motors and fan units. We put these together to form a unit that was powered by the Lister diesel whilst out on the road and, in the evening at the depot, they would plug into the electricity supply. Adams were very much at the forefront of this in the early 1960s.

Trevor Sales

I started to work for Adams Butter in the mid 1950s. The first day I ever went out on my own was in a little 30cwt vehicle, YRF something, it was. Everyone went on that to start with. I went to Mrs Coe in Langford Street, Leek and I was there before she opened. With small deliveries we took money sometimes and this was my first one. I'd got a receipt book and I made it all out while I was waiting for her to open up. I hadn't got any stamps but I knew she sold them. So when she came out and signed she gave me a stamp and I put it on. Well she had a go at me. 'You don't do that - you sign over the stamp!' She was OK after that; she enjoyed telling me off, I think.

My second delivery was to Alexander's shop at Ipstones. We delivered and I noticed she had some billy cans hanging in the shop so I bought one. She said 'Just hang on a minute; I'll wash it out for you'. When she came out and gave it back to me it was full of hot tea.

I worked on four wheelers mainly. I did take an artic now and again but with being a single bloke I wanted to get back to go down the pub with my mates. I remember I had a TK Bedford which had a special engine in - experimental, they said. I was told to drive it as hard as possible. Every Friday morning the chief men from Bedford would be in the garage waiting for me, all the garage doors open, so they could inspect it - brakes steaming and everything, you know. It had a blower on and it was unheard of in them days, in a diesel anyway. I was like a test pilot.

I remember I was in Birmingham delivering one day and a man came up to me. He said 'Are you from Head Office?' I said I was. He said 'Wait there a minute, I'll be back'. He came back with a little box and he hands it to me. I open the box and there's a finger in it that he's found in some butter. I made a note of his details and took the finger back to the office!

We changed over from the old log books to the continental ones, this is before the tachograph, I can't remember the year. Well, I'd never studied this new log book. Anyway, because some of us lived nearby, the night loaders would leave the vans up here for us. They'd left my van in the boss's parking space on this particular day and he wanted to park his car, so I set off straight away without doing this log. Just outside Hereford there's a big lay-by and I pulled on and was studying this log book and filling it in. A policeman pulls up on a motorbike. He said 'Are these the new log books? 'I had to be honest and said 'I'm just filling it in' and he said 'Can I get in with you and we'll fill it in together'. So we did.

Me and John are cousins - John's dad was Harry. A little tale about our uncle Jack Fernyhough: At the top of Ladderedge, where it levels out there's a farm on the left. You can

Trevor Sales standing in front of his Bedford c.1965.

just see it at the side of the road and there's a little driveway down to it. Uncle Jack lived there and he always had horses. Anyway, he was talked into getting a tractor. Well, he's driving this tractor and he's shouting 'Whoah!' to it to stop and pulling on the steering wheel. He drove it through the wall one day into the road, turned it around and drove back through a different part of the wall. He had it all built up and Yotter (Johnny Scragg) drove through it again. Uncle Jack said 'I know what caused it; he was changing gear on the move!' They were good days.

I remember when I had a knocking 'diff' on my vehicle and for a few days it was getting worse and worse. I kept complaining and they said they'd got one ordered but in the end they said 'we may have to put an old one in'. So, this morning I set off and it was quiet as anything. I stopped in the same lay-by in Hereford where that policeman had stopped me with the log book. Just before I pulled in there was such a bang. Then, knock, knock, knock. Well, I thought that it was the old diff causing the trouble. Anyway, I rang up and they said they'd send Roy Lancaster and Pete Middleton. While I was waiting for them to arrive I took the back plate off and it was a brand new diff they'd put in. I'd let all the oil out as well. Anyway, I'm staring at this brand new diff when they pulled up behind me. Well, it wasn't the diff, it was one of the inside wheels, the rim had burst out and it was hitting the springs. They said 'It's a long way to come just to change a wheel'.

Some of the people I remember who worked on Adams Butter were my father, Denis Sales; Reubin Gibson; Bernard Peach; Bernard 'Pongo' Waring and George 'Gunker' Keates who kept everything spotless clean.

Towards the end, I left because of Tesco. They wouldn't unload us and all that business. There was a company called Blower Brothers that had shops all over the Lancashire area. It was a good company and Tesco took them over. We'd pull up outside and wheel the stuff in to the butter counter, no trouble at all. I remember I'd got to deliver to one of these shops at Blackpool, right opposite the ABC theatre. I'd got a load for them but just before I left Leek they said 'Hang on for 15 minutes, we've got a box of unsalted for them'. Anyway, when I got there I did what I always did and wheeled the butter in. They were the same girls at the counter and two old ladies were being served. When the assistant saw me she said 'Oh, he's here now, I'll ask him. Have you got any unsalted on?' I said 'Yes, it's for you, I'll go and fetch it'. I remember it was twenty past three.

Then a voice says 'Oh, no you won't'. It was the manager and he says 'Not at this time of day, I don't accept deliveries at this time of day'. So I told the girl 'You'll have to tell those two old ladies they can't have their unsalted because that big baby-faced devil (he was right mard looking) won't let me unload it'. He heard me and said 'There's no need for personal comments'. I had to take it out and put it back on the van. I rang our firm up and said 'Get my cards ready because I'm not coming here again'. We were stopping overnight and I waited until 3.30 the next day and went back to deliver, expecting him to turn me away again, but he didn't.

John Lancaster

When I started in the 1950s they had seven vehicles. I was a driver's mate at first and then I went on to shunting. I worked for Adams Butter for forty six years. The vehicles were all petrol originally then they started buying Perkins engines and that was fatal. Instead of nipping off in a morning and getting going we'd be there with a calor gas pump first and then a piece of wire with a rag on dipped in something inflammable and you'd have to light it and take the air filter off. This was a two man job. The other bloke would be turning the engine over and then you'd

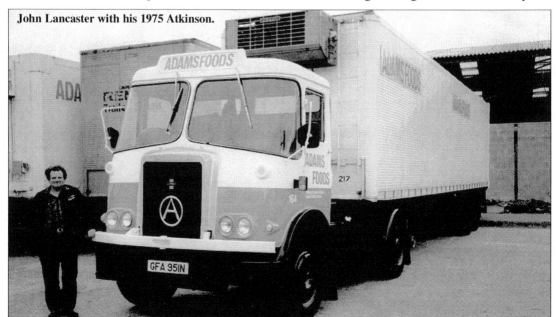

John Lancaster with his 1975 Atkinson.

put the flame in to get it going. It was alright once you'd got going. I remember once when the rag shot out and went down the engine. It jammed it all up and Johnno said 'There's only one thing to do with that, tow it up to the top of Hulme, turn it around and let it go down. It got halfway down the bank and suddenly came to life. Stuff was coming out of the back like snow.

I started with a 40 cwt Bedford when I came out of the army in the 1950s. I was going up to Newcastle upon Tyne one day and got pulled up by the police and done for speeding. It was a brand new vehicle. They pulled me into the side and there was no tax disc in as it was still in the post. There was hell up about it. I was overtaking an eight wheeler on a dual carriageway and they pulled me up and did me - £20. I went up to pay it in Darlington and said 'This is a bit stiff, isn't it?' I told them what I was doing, overtaking the eight wheeler. I said 'If I was speeding, he was speeding'. 'It's you we're talking about and you hadn't got a tax disc in'. They simply wouldn't listen. 'You were lucky we didn't do you for more than we did!' I said 'You've done me enough!'

When I had my first artic I had John Fearns with me as driver's mate and he used to get down in the seat and he'd be fast asleep in no time. I used to have a stick and I used to hit him on the arm to wake him up. Anyway, I did it two or three times and then he started to put a lump of wood up his coat sleeve so he wouldn't feel it.

I can remember as a boy going in the old Sentinel vehicles - my Uncle Denis (Sales) used to drive one, as did Graham Barber. They were petrol wagons, not steam. They only had one steam one and my dad drove that. He was running to London in it all the time.

I remember being stuck one May on top of Royal Cottage, just past the Roaches. The snow was so bad they came and fetched us in again. We also got snowed in at Grimsby - six or seven vehicles unable to move for a week. A lot of the driver's used to stop at a place we called Ma Maddison's in Grimsby - it was a regular stop for the Adams' drivers. Everyone knew Ma Maddison.

Les Bailey

I started working at Adams Butter in the latter part of 1961. I was on artics from day one. I was on day deliveries to different parts of the country but later went on to London trunk in late 1962. Up until that time they had employed four drivers based in Rugby but when the motorway had got up to Crick they decided to run direct from Leek.

There were three of us on two lorries; Joe Hampton and Maurice Murfin were the others. Each driver did ten trips in three weeks and we ran to Blackfriars in the City. Sometimes, when there was more work, they would have three trunk lorries a night so we'd have an extra man. The entire trip took us about 12 hours there and back including break times. We took packet butter down and brought bulk butter back. We were always fully loaded both ways.

On 29th November 1966 I had a very serious accident and was hospitalised for quite a few months. The accident happened on the northbound carriageway of the M1, near Toddington, Bedfordshire. It was just after eight o clock in the morning when I hit a lorry carrying a load of steel girders. This lorry was in front of me in the first lane of the motorway when its engine seized up and, for whatever reason, I ran into the back of it. The steel girders were longer than the trailer they were on and they penetrated through my cab and into the load of butter behind. There's about a three foot gap between the cab and the front of the trailer. One length of steel went between my legs and the others went straight past me. I would have been killed if any of them had hit me. The cab was crushed beyond recognition. Apparently, I was trapped for nearly two and a half hours as firemen and men from a nearby garage fought to cut me out. I was drifting in and out of consciousness during this time. There was a doctor there and I was obviously under sedation because of the severity of the injuries.

I was taken to Luton and Dunstable hospital where I was in intensive care for about three weeks. I had very serious stomach injuries and I'd broken my femur on my left leg and my tibia on my right. They didn't expect me to live. I must have been coming round one night and I put my hand to my chin and felt my whiskers. I hadn't had a shave. I asked the night sister if there was any chance of having a mirror and a razor. I remember she was a German lady and she

Les Bailey's AEC Mandator with Egreman cab, after the accident on the M1, 1966.

broke down in tears. I couldn't make out what was wrong with her. She said 'That's it. That's the turning point. You're going to make it'.

The Adams family was very good. They provided a car to bring my parents down to see me every week; I wasn't married at the time and was still living at home. It was also available for other family and friends and the hospital allowed the Adams drivers to come and park their trucks there at any time so they could visit. I wasn't short of visitors. Obviously, because of the distance involved, my visitors couldn't come to see me in the evenings. However, a lady named Hilda Johnson who was a seamstress at the hospital and her husband, Sam, started chatting to me when they were visiting someone else and we became life-long friends. They lived at Dunstable and Sam was a manager at Vauxhall Motors in those days. Their two children, Peter and Lesley also came in to see me. Unfortunately, Sam fell from a ladder some years ago and died. I'm still in touch with Hilda - we exchange Christmas cards and sometimes speak on the phone.

I was in hospital at Dunstable for four months and had to learn to walk again because I'd been in plaster from my toe right up my left leg to my waist. And, of course, the other leg was broken too. I was walking with two sticks when I was sent back to the North Staffs Hospital. I spent a week

or so there and then went home although I had to keep going back for physio. I'd also had a colostomy due to my stomach injuries. Dr Trafford at the North Staffs reversed that for me and I've been ok ever since. I was thirty when the accident happened and I suppose I survived because I was young and fit.

I was off work for about fourteen months. I started back in the early part of 1968. I went straight back on the job I'd done before, on the trunk to London again. I was ok when I got back in the wagon, it never really affected me. By this time Adams Butter had built the new factory at Waltham Abbey and the journey wasn't quite as far. I did that for a while and then I went on nights in the garage for about a year before going back on normal road deliveries.

Les Bailey with his DAF 2800 c.1987, at Roach Foods, Bugle, Cornwall.

The Sentinel Steamer (reg CRE 202, 1935) which H Lancaster and G Woodings drove.

All photos Alan Smith Collection

ABOVE:
An impressive line-up of Adams vehicles. Taken at Birchall, just outside Leek c.1950

Albion, reg no 196 JRF, pictured outside Adams London office, No.1 London Bridge c.1955.

BELFIELDS ROAD SERVICES:

Johnny Harding

George Belfield started the business in the days of horses and carts. Charlie, his brother, later joined him. They had three sisters, Jane, Emily and Cissie. Jane married Ty Walley and Emily, my grandmother, married Harry Harding. Cissie never married. All three families, the Belfields, the Walleys and the Hardings were shareholders in the business.

Harry Harding. Taken in the 1930s in Hanley Park.

The business operated from a place in Dale Hall in Burslem at the top of St Paul's Street. They also had a shop, a sort of general store that sold everything. It had an' outdoor' for selling beer. Customers would come along with a jug to put the beer in. I can remember the kegs were all on proper stands. In those days they used to sell big bottles of beer with screw tops on so people would buy one of these, take it home and when it was empty they'd come back and have it filled with draught beer. Belfields also had a coal business running alongside the regular transport, so they would be delivering coal as well. All the family were involved in the business in one way or another and it was all operated from this place in Dale Hall.

There was always a lot going on. When grandma was alive she used to do breakfasts for all the drivers. They would sit in the back kitchen eating bacon, eggs, sausage and tomatoes with cut bread and as much tea as they could drink. She'd have this great big teapot on the table. Me, Dad and Stuart would come in at about 9.30 in the morning after we'd done what we had to do and Stuart's mum would do his breakfast and my grandma would do ours. Grandma would also do the dinners for them all. It was a big property, really. The office was in the front room. When Grandma died in 1966 Cissie took over the running of the shop.

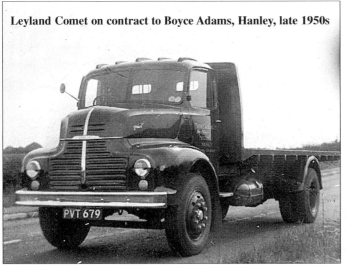

Leyland Comet on contract to Boyce Adams, Hanley, late 1950s

When transport was denationalized George set up again as Belfields Road Services, but it was still the three families involved. This would be about 1954. I can remember going with my dad and Arthur Shaw down to BRS at Dudley where we bought KEH 404, an ERF and a six wheel Maudsley. Arthur drove the Maudsley and my dad drove KEH. John Belfield had the Boyce Adams wagon on contract. Charlie was in the office running things. We didn't have anyone doing repairs at that time, they

Norman Harding and Dennis James in the yard, late 1950s.

did everything themselves.

The business started to grow and they bought another ERF from Bassetts at Tipton, KTU 434 and two six wheel Leyland twin steers - XEH 101 and YEH 387. These were brand new from Newcastle Motors in Brunswick Street, Newcastle before they moved to where Tesco is now in Trent Vale. Stuart Walley drove one and Arthur Shaw the other. Then my dad had a brand new Leyland Comet, VVT 502.

I can remember we had a few Albions off Warwick Motors in Copeland Street, Stoke. We had the first six wheel Reivers from them. Leylands and Albions were separate then; Warwicks sold Albions and Newcastle Motors sold Leylands. Shortlands were the Dodge people. I remember the first artic we had was from Beechs.

In the 1960s they probably had seven or eight vehicles. When Charlie died John Belfield took over the running of the company. Dad and Stuart wouldn't have anything to do with that side, they preferred to drive. At its height the business had about fifteen wagons. All the transport companies in Stoke were doing the same stuff - clay or flints back up for the pot banks. Belfields was a good company to work for; there was always a waiting list of people wanting driving jobs. There wasn't the stiff competition like there is now between the different companies. If you were broken down people would stop to help you - not just one person, there would be several. I can remember when I was courting my wife, Gwen; she lived in a flat on the main road at Rugeley. I used to call in to see her and other drivers would be coming past and think the wagon was broken down so they'd stop. One after the other! You'd also see a lot of 'transhipping' going on at The Woodley at one o clock in the morning before everyone set off down country. Someone would say, 'I'll take that for you' and someone else would say 'I'll take that' and they would transfer stuff from one wagon on to another to save everybody running all round London.

We had some good lads working for us: Jake Smith, Colin Leake, Ray Kennedy, Graham Newton, Georgie Bryant, Ray Gould, Joey Stringer, Freddie Leese, Albert Bentley, Siddie Turner, Roy Corbet and Johnny Proctor. All the wagons had a name written on them: Maggie May, Scheherazade, The Impatient Virgin (Billy Jones drove that), Crimson Pirate, and Johnny One Note (John Belfield was a big Frank Sinatra fan).

All the wagons were painted at Hudson and Boultons at Bucknall and sign-written properly with gold leaf. The trucks were maroon and then John decided to have a grey stripe around them. The sign-writing was done by a bloke named Charlie from Hudson and Boultons. If one of the trucks got smashed up there was a bloke there, Bill Shone, who could do anything with fibreglass. I've known a driver to come in on a Saturday morning with half a cab missing on an ERF and they've been able to go back on the road on the Sunday night - not painted but repaired.

Bob Abbotts was a good electrician who did work for us. Tommy Gater was a driver who came off the road to work in the garage with John Wheat. My dad used to do a bit in the garage as well as he was in the REME in the army. Arthur Shaw used to repair all the sideboards on the trailers and Freddie Leese would paint them. All these odd jobs would be done on a Monday or a Wednesday when it was quiet; the trucks went down country on Sunday night and did not come back until Tuesday. The only wagons you had in the yard on those days were those on coal because they used to go down and back in the night. John Belfield was a stickler for cleanliness so the wagons, and trailers had to be washed off three times a week. We'd wash them off with DAZ and a brush.

As I say, we used to do clay and flints. Clay was harder work. People don't realise the places we used to have to go. When you went to Royal Doultons, for instance, you couldn't stand up to shovel it off. You were bent double because you used to bang your head on the roof. Then there was 'Grindley Hotel' where we used to deliver clay. There were two Grindley factories but Grindley Hotel in Scotia Road was where they made all the hotel ware. When you went there you used to back alongside this window. Then you had to take the window frame out, throw the clay through the hole and, if you'd got twenty ton on, you'd have to climb inside and throw everything you've thrown in further back, so you could get the other half load in. Then you had to put the frame back in. To be honest, if you couldn't use a shovel in the Potteries, you couldn't get a job. No matter who you went to work for, whatever you brought back was usually for the pottery industry and it had got to be thrown off with a shovel.

At odd times we used to bring 'fondue' out of West Thurrock. All the fireplace firms around the Potteries used it to put tiles in the frames. It was black, heat resistant cement. Anyway, one of our blokes brings this ten ton of fondue in on a Saturday morning and couldn't unload it. John Belfield needed the trailer so they decided to unload it and store it in the garage. So there's a lad on the back of the wagon putting it to the side and the blokes are carrying it in. We had a lad, John Cooke, a big, raw boned man as strong as a horse. Joey Stringer is on the back of the wagon and says, 'Can you carry two bags of fondue, Cookie?' He says, 'Yeah, no problem'. So he's got two 1 cwt bags on his shoulder and carries them in. Not to be beaten, this other guy named Peter says 'put me two on, Joe'. Anyway, he struggles with these two bags. So the next time Johnny Cooke carries three bags in. So Peter's got to do three and really struggles. John Belfield says, 'If you drop any of that and burst it you'll have the sack.' So then Johnny does four and Peter's at the side of the wagon, he's got three on his shoulder and Joey drops the last bag and Peter just sank down the side of the wagon into the gutter with four bags of fondue around him.

We used to load a lot of stuff out of Liverpool because John had a contact that used to work for a clearing house there. Anyway, this chap finished and started working on his own under Belfields Road Services, Liverpool. It wasn't a partnership or anything he just needed the name. Anyway, I'm at the docks one day picking up a load of oil rig pipes that had come from the Middle East for Great Yarmouth. I came back into the yard and went in to his little office in Cotton Street at about half past five. He said, 'Any room on that trailer?' I said. 'No, I've only got about a foot at the end'. He said that Liverpool Bacon had rung up and had got three tons of boxed bacon to go into Keeley and Tongues at Harlow and it had got to be there for 7.00am. He told me to go over to Birkenhead and see if I could get it on. I said, 'How am I going to get it on?' He said, 'Those pipes are hollow aren't they? Just keep shoving it up the pipes as much as you can and stack the rest up the back'. And that's what I did.

There aren't the characters around nowadays. We had this bloke named Jake Smith who worked for us and he had this ERF and from the day it came Jake moaned about this wagon.

Every day. The steering was heavy or it wouldn't pull. He would always start with 'Dust ere?' We had another bloke who worked for us who always had to have a sub. The blokes in those days used to do three trips and they'd be paid £55. This bloke would come in on a Tuesday morning and say, 'Anything in the sub tin, John?' And he'd have a tenner. Then it was the same again on a Thursday night. So Saturday morning he was only going home with £35. The following Tuesday he was skint again.

The directors gradually reduced the number of wagons they ran and eventually decided to close. Dave Unwin bought the last of the vehicles. I still work in transport and my son, Martin, is also a driver making him the fourth generation to be involved in haulage.

John Harding with son Martin who is also a driver. 2001.

Ryan Tarrant Jnr

My dad was 39 when he died. I'm next to the oldest in the family and I was about fifteen then. Everybody who knew him said he was a grafter. It didn't matter what was asked of him he went out and did it. Others would go down to the south coast and park up but my old man would go down, tip and come back in a day so he could get an extra trip in.

Even though we were a big family we always had a holiday. He was a good dad. Very strict, though. As soon as we heard his truck coming round the corner you could hear a pin drop

Ryan Tarrant Sr who died when his lorry was in a collision on 6th May, 1969 at Grendon on the A5.

in our house. If it wasn't that way he'd play hell with us. It was only in the last few years of his life that we noticed a change in him. He packed up smoking just before he died.

It was such a shock for everyone when Dad died. They say there wasn't a mark on him, we weren't allowed to see him in his coffin.

I can remember that we each had to go down to Macclesfield when we came of age 21. We had to go to the building society to get our share of the money that had been collected for us by people in the haulage business. It was lovely to have this. Stuart Walley knew my dad better than anyone and he used to come up to our house in an open top Sunbeam and take me, Stephen and the twins out on a Sunday afternoon. Ronnie Joynson and my dad were the best of mates.

All the Belfield drivers liked Dad; it's quite emotional sometimes when people who knew him tell me about him. My brother Stephen worked for John Belfield for a time and when I was old enough he offered me a job as well.

Johnny standing in front of YEH387, a
Leyland Steer purchased new from
Newcastle Motors.

RIGHT:
Johnny beside KEH 404 outside the
garage in Globe Street c.1951.

**The Albions in this line-up
were all purchased from
Warwick Motors in Stoke. The
ERFs were purchased
from Beech's.**

Shown across 2 pages

ABOVE:
Johnny with Bedford LEH 911.
This vehicle did coal, then had
a meat van on for the Fatstock
Marketing Corporation.
(FMC).

An 1940s advert in
a church magazine.

The vehicle on the left (KEH 404) was the first ERF bought after de-nationalization.

All Photos J Harding Collection

A night out. Front L-R: John Belfield, Norman Harding, Lilian Harding, ? June Owen (standing), June Belfield.
Back: Dennis James, Frank Philips, Jean Wood (Peter Foden's private secretary), Stuart Walley, ?, Rita Phillips,
Mrs Dennis James, Ernie Owen and Mr and Mrs Dave Shipton. 1960s.

J HAYDON & SONS: Stan Jukes

Somerfield car park in Biddulph was a field belonging to Haydon's farm when I was young. Our house, which was the police station in the early 1900s, backed on to this field. I was a toddler when I first started going there. They used to milk cows and they had a slaughterhouse. There was also another slaughterhouse where the Somerfields building is now. As I got older I used to drive tractors, did farming and one thing and another, and they'd got these cattle wagons. They didn't do general haulage, just cattle.

The business was established in 1918 with the old man and his three sons: Jack Jr, Tom and Fred. Frank was the youngest but he didn't have anything to do with the lorries; he was on the farm when he came out of the army and he died when he was only in his thirties. He was married to Hilda Bailey, now Sheldon, who has Brammer's shoe shop.

From the age of eight or nine, I'd be riding up and down in these wagons. I'd be going to cattle markets and coming back. They were old Albions, we used to have to swing them to start. Then every Saturday morning and Sundays I used to go down washing them out so I could drive 'em in the yard. I used to have to stand up to reach the pedals. That's how I learnt to drive.

I drove a wagon when I was fifteen; I wasn't supposed to but Arthur Copeland let me have a go with him many a time. Then I started doing a bit in the slaughterhouse. Haydons rented the slaughterhouse to local butchers and I was working for them as well. I wasn't getting paid a lot of money but getting a tremendous amount of experience on how to pull motors apart and mend 'em and drive these lorries.

Haydon & Sons went on to be pretty well known and had about a dozen lorries. The drivers used to go out in a morning and each lorry would go with about five or six, or even ten collections to go to Uttoxeter, Leek, Crewe, Newcastle, or Congleton markets and take the animals in and unload them. Then they had to wait there all flaming day til they'd all been sold and hopefully there would be somebody who wanted stuff taking home. With a bit of luck some of the big people like Longmans, the meat wholesalers, would buy two or three wagon loads. The wagons used to go to Sheffield, Manchester, Banbury,

Jack Haydon Jr in front of Bedford with younger brother Frank.

Rochdale, Oldham and all over the place, really. They used to go to Boston, Lincs where there was a Dutchman who had a big holding yard and he bought all these cows. He'd have them down there and fatten 'em up and then he'd send them over to Holland.

Haydons set up a bit of a company with Harold Wain who came from Milton or Baddeley Green. He'd worked for the Albion agents, Warwick Motors, in Stoke. He used to have a blue Standard 10 van with H Wain on it in gold writing and I used to drive it around the yard. We used to go to such as Warwick Motors or Tom Byatt's in Fenton for spares for these wagons. Harold Wain was a very clever man with regards to engines. He never swore; if he hit his thumb with a hammer he'd say, 'Ooh, the Mary Ellen'. He lived in Haydon's old farm house when he first came to Biddulph because I flitted him in the cattle wagon. And I also flitted Frank Machin; Frank and his wife, Eunice are both dead now.

On a Saturday it was Malpass Market, Chester Road. I used to go with Harry Worthy - he still comes to Biddulph most days. Haydons had one Ford Trader and they ended up putting an Albion engine in it. Harry drove this lorry and they had a Bedford S Type off Charlie Myatt at Gratton, a calf dealer. They used to take his calves to Mold auction. Every day through the school holidays I was with them. I started going out on the wagons when I was twelve from about 1957 onwards.

I also went to Malpass auction with Jack Longman; he had a Ford Zephyr then. He used to live at Digg Lake Farm at Buglawton. Longman's slaughterhouses then were at the back of Woolworth's in Congleton. Only a little tiny place and they used to go up there with ten or a dozen or more cows in a wagon, turn 'em in and Cyril, who was a foreman, only got one eye, would go round and go bang, bang, bang and they'd all go down. And then Sammy Bantick would come out and cut their throats. Now you only do one at a time.

Anyway, Jack Longman didn't take a wagon to Malpass in case he didn't buy anything - but invariably he did. And he would buy one, two or three loads, sometimes four if they were very cheap. Then I would sort 'em all out into different pens and ring Haydon's and ask them to send one or two or whatever wagons. I'd tell them how many cows or sheep and they'd send

L-R: Tom Haydon, Fred Haydon, Frank Haydon, Jack Haydon Sr, Jack Haydon Jr. with their new Albion Clydesdale.

the appropriate lorries and that would be Saturday dinner time and we would still be messing about by Saturday night. That's how the cattle job was, you started early in the morning and you couldn't finish until eight or nine because of the auctions. Then they had to deliver the cattle to where they had to go. As I say, sometimes it would be Sheffield which is a long way in them old Albions, thirty miles an hour going up Solomon's Hollow, as fast as a snail. Haydons never really paid me a penny, I don't think. They taught me everything I know. I learned how to do a bit of spannering, how to do my killing, drive a wagon, drive a tractor and I learnt a bit of farming.

I can remember one of the drivers, it may have been Sid Unwin, always driving along singing hymns - 'What a friend I have in Jesus'. And old Jack Ash, a little man, they called him Squeak. His brother had a cattle wagon of his own. Jack had the first three-decker at Haydons. It had a maroon body on it. I went to Oswestry with him and I'd be sitting there and these bonnets used to get red hot. If they'd got petrol in you couldn't sit on the beggars, they were that hot. Anyway, Jack had no teeth and he'd be driving along and he'd put his tongue up his nose. We used to laugh. Denis Mountain is married to Jack Ash's daughter and we have a laugh many a time about her dad. Pearl and Laura, his daughters, were in service to the people in Henshall Hall. They were fancy wenches. When I was about fifteen they'd be about twenty - by god, they'd fetch ducks off water!

Joe Brown worked for Haydons pretty much all his life. We used to go to Walters' Butchers in Milton. 'Gunner' (Walters) had a piece of ground at the back of the shop and when we'd brought his cattle from the auction we turned 'em in there. He killed at Hanley Abattoir, I think, but when they closed he started coming to Haydens. I'd be fifteen, maybe more, and on a Sunday morning Gunner would come with a dozen or more cattle and he could hardly fit 'em in. Twenty or thirty sheep and ten or a dozen pigs because he was doing a bit of wholesaling to other butchers as well as killing for himself. I used to go down on a Sunday morning and then we'd finish at about 1.00 or half past and go down to The Oak. One day we came out, down the steps and who's waiting there? Me dad! 'What at thay doin' 'ere?' Then a smack right across the ear-hole. 'Get tha sen across wom'.

I remember Harold Massey who used to drive for them. They had a Clydesdale, with all polished wood in the cab, 673 BVT, it was beautiful - the only new one they ever had and Harold drove it. A lovely wagon. The drivers I used to go with were Harry Worthy from Norton who went to work for them after he came out of the army, and Harry Lomas. Harry Lomas died last year. He was a cattle dealer and a character. He could talk! He'd tell you some tales. He used to come in on a morning with a white enamel billy can, cold tea and offer you something to eat. 'Dost want a round o' beef, Jukey?' I'd be about 12 or 13 and I'd say yes. My mother and dad didn't know I'd gone; I'd sneak out of the house, go over the wall and be gone. They wouldn't see me til midnight. Anyway, he'd put that much mustard on this sandwich and it'd be that hot. Oh, by god, you knew you'd had it. And I swear he only put that much on so you wouldn't have another.

I was down Haydons one morning - there was Harry Worthy, Harry Lomas, John Holland from Kidsgrove, Arthur Copeland. Arthur's dad, Dick, helped Haydon's when they set up; he was the first driver they set on. Anyway, this particular morning I go down and go in the office. I went like I was a worker, but I wasn't and I never had any money or snappin' - I'd go with whoever would look after me. And they'd give you a fag as well. I was going with Harry Worthy. I said, 'Are we right?' Then Jack Haydon comes out: 'Ey up, Stanley, I dunner want you to go with Harry Worthy'. I asked him why and he said he wanted me to go with a bloke I didn't like. I said, 'I aren't goin' with him, I can't abide him'. He wouldn't give you anything. If he'd got twenty sandwiches he wouldn't give you a crumb. He was that tight.

Jack Haydon said I'd got to go with him and he'd got ten pick-ups for the FMC (The Fat Stock Marketing Company) and it was all over England. They used to have collections of pigs and used to take them to a slaughterhouse, whether it be here or further afield. The farmer would have a contract with the FMC. He said he'd got these 10 collections all over the place. It was a nuisance job trying to keep everything separate and you had to slap 'em and put this number on them. Anyway, I said I wouldn't go and turned round and started marching up the road. I got to where the police station was and all of a sudden a voice shouts, '*Ay up, come 'ere'*. I turned round and went back down and Jack Haydon said, '*Wut go now?'* and he gave me a pound note and that's the only pound note he ever gave me.

Over the years I'd carted hay for him; I'd gone out and cut kale in winter and your hands were that cold you couldn't tell you'd got fingers, in an old Fordson tractor. I'd swilled wagons off until I was frozen. The silage pit that's still there now, opposite Armit's yard, well, me and Peter Robinson barrowed all one summer holiday. In those days Armit's yard was the council tip and we barrowed bricks and broken bricks across the road from the tip to make Hayden's sileage tip. We mixed the concrete by hand. We would only be 14. We did it all for nothing, not a penny. Mrs Haydon would give you some sandwiches and she used to make ginger beer that used to blow the top off the bottle.

I have a picture of when they built the two houses where Fred Haydon lives now. The chimney's been taken off and I'm on this picture when I was 12, standing on the roof passing bricks up to the builder. Jack Nixon of Nixon and Rutter was the builder.

I can remember Fred Haydon sitting in the wagon, 'Spell OXO, Stanley'. I'd ask why and he'd say 'Just spell it'. 'O-X-O'. 'Aye, that's right. Now, spell it backerts'. So I'd say, 'O-X-O'. No, that's fronterts'. Then he'd say, 'How many beans make five?' The answer would be, 'A bean, a bean a half a bean, a half a bean, a bean, a bean'. Daft things like that. And they'd send you up the shop, not for 10 Woodbines but for 10 very nice Woodbines. 'Don't bring the ordinary ones'. And you'd go in and ask for them, like a fool. 'Fetch a quarter of Lovell's everlasting mints', that was another one. We went in and asked for them. It was so silly but really funny, you know, when you look back.

Anyway, I left school and went to Browns in Hanley, a big firm, and got myself a job in their slaughterhouse. My dad wanted me to go in the pit. I worked with Ian Adams there. He was a couple of years older than me. I've got two little blue marks, like tattoos, on my arm. I got those off him. With pigs you had a slapper with little pins in and you'd put it in ink and you slapped the pig and it put a number on so you could tell which pig was which. Anyway, we were playing around, fighting and he hit me with it and it has never come out. I worked at Browns until I was 21 and then I started on my own running a grocery business and then a butcher's shop, with a slaughterhouse at the back, in Biddulph.

By the time I was thirty I was divorcing and I packed up butchering and went driving a lorry. I started at a firm in Tunstall in a six wheeler ergomatic Leyland or AEC or something. That didn't last long. Then I had one of those big round cab ERFs. We used to go to Middlewich on a Saturday morning, put about twenty ton of salt on, come back to the yard, take the twenty ton of salt off, go back and put another twenty ton on, come back to Tunstall and put the first twenty ton on top of the second twenty ton and take it to Matheson's meats in London.

I got going into the Woodley Cafe at Barlaston on the A34. It was open 24 hours, and you never left Stoke without stopping there and you never came back without calling for a brew. Everybody, all the trunkers, congregated there at about midnight for a one o clock start. Anyway, I got talking to Kane Mayer and he told me to go up to see 'Daley' at Beresford's and he set me on. Ray Swindells took me out in one of those old Mickey Mouse Fodens, 12 speed - I didn't know what they were at the time. Anyway, I started going abroad with Beresfords to Italy, France, Switzerland - all over Europe, pretty much. I really enjoyed it; I can speak French and Italian quite well.

In 1986 I went back to butchering when I bought a business on Biddulph High Street, number 76, selling meat and later we had a deli counter as well. I'd seen a lot while I was travelling and wanted to bring 'a taste of Italy' to Biddulph. I also opened a cake shop in the High Street and we had another shop in Smallthorne. At one time I employed about 14 people.

I can remember once, when I was driving in Italy for Beresfords, seeing this man sitting on a chair in the middle of a street - he was stopping workmen from digging the road up. He

wouldn't move and they couldn't do anything. One Saturday morning I was in the shop when council workers started doing the same right outside. Such a racket. I'd got people queuing outside; we couldn't hear ourselves speak. Anyway, I took a chair outside and did exactly the same as this Italian had done. Robert Orme from Kaye's sweet shop came out and sat with me. They couldn't do anything. The police came but we refused to move and *The Sentinel* and *Biddulph Chronicle* sent a photographer. In the end, the workmen had to pack up and go home.

L-R: Joe Brereton, Les Elkin, Dennis Clowes. Both Joe and Dennis are cattle dealers.

Tom Haydon.

David Haydon, 1991

If for the council you do work,
With JCB and shovel.
Don't dig a hole outside Stan's shop
Or you will get in trouble.

Stanley is the Master Butcher,
To sell meat is his goal.
But he was none too pleased
When he went outside to find the hole.

The noise had first attracted Stan,
He couldn't even speak.
So Stan got out his strongest chair
And dangled in his feet.

Longton Crane Hire couldn't come,
To move Stan from his chair.
So Council and the Policemen
Had to leave him there.

With tea in hand and dog on knee
Old Stanley just sat there.
The workmen had to fill the hole
And go home in despair.

This little rhyme is just a joke,
I hope you will agree.
If Stan and Council don't agree
The one in trouble - is me!

This is the poem David Haydon wrote about Stan's protest. Stan had it framed and has it on his wall at home.

All photos F. Haydon and S Jukes Collections

Stan's protest: L-R: Robert Orme, owner of Kays Sweet Shop (now Wrights Pies), Stan with his dog, Pepe, and Mrs Josie Wain of Wain's TV Shop.

ERNEST E OWEN - ERNIE OWEN

Paul Owen

My dad started in haulage when he came out of the army and bought an ex-army Bedford truck. He didn't have a yard at first - he operated from my nan and grandad's council house in Vernon Avenue, Audley. My grandad was a manager at Downings Tiles at Knutton and tiles were needed in London to repair the war damage. So dad started by ferrying these tiles down to London. When that work started to wane he began transporting salt, in bags, for Palmer Mann at Middlewich. Again, he was travelling to London.

Obviously, the wagon needed to be earning both ways so it was necessary to find loads back to Stoke. At this time there were quite a few people doing the same work: John Heathcote, John Belfield from Burslem and A & H Davey - they were all bringing return loads of flints for the pottery industry so it was salt or tiles down and flints back.

By the early 1960s he probably had about 16 trucks. They were mostly rigids but then we started doing artics and that's where I came in; it fell to me to convert the rigids into artics. It was such a performance, we were cutting these things up and making tractor units out of eight wheelers and all sorts. I remember those horrible BTC four-in-line trailers - really horrible but they were all you could get at the time.

Anyway, the flint job was very cut-throat and the rates kept dropping. A turning point for my dad was when the price for a load of flints from Dartford back to the Potteries got down to a £1 a ton. The flints would come up on flat trailers, not tippers, and you shovelled them off at this end. So my job was to run round in a van with about six blokes in the back with shovels to various pot banks around the Potteries. Three days a week we'd be going out and shovelling 20 ton of flints off - perhaps six or eight wagons at a time.

It would be a six o clock start, do the shovelling and then dash off to Sandbach to load salt. Some of it was table salt in boxes and some in bags. None of it was on pallets so it was all handball. Then back to the yard. Of course, you wouldn't always have the right deliveries on the right vehicles so you had to unsheet them - it was all ropes and sheets then - and you'd take this off and take that off. You could be there until 1.00 in the morning, re-jigging all the loads so they were in the right order for delivery. This was normal for the job at the time.

I can remember there used to be a company called Dolby's, their factory was situated where the canal runs alongside the A500 where the two underpasses are now. It had been there for donkey's years. The canal was one side and Dolby's place was on the other side. The only way you could get in off the road was to reverse in. So you'd got a forty foot trailer backed in and all these flints had got to go on to a raised platform ready to go into the bottle kiln. Well, you can shovel them at the start, you can throw them a bit but when it gets like ten feet away you've got to carry them- every shovelful, up and down, up and down. We had three trailers there with twenty tons on; that's sixty tons of flint to come off by shovel, three times a week. Hard work.

Another place was Richards of Adderley Green. It was a brand new factory but where they needed the flints you still couldn't go in with a tipper because it was under the building. What they used to do there was use a JCB, a Chayside, and they would drop the sides and push them off with the machine which made it a lot quicker and easier. But as you pushed the flints some of them would roll and break the floorboards of the trailer. Anyway, when it got to £1 a ton my dad said *'That's it. I'm not carrying flints. I've done that, I'm finished'*. Then he cut the side boards off every trailer so he couldn't carry them any more.

After that, we started running to Scotland carrying bricks from Downings and bringing fire bricks back. This was probably the mid 1960s and the best period for the business financially. In the period between 1965 and 1970 one of my dad's yardsticks was that if a truck didn't earn £1000 a week it didn't go out of the yard. It was £300+ per trip, that's what it had to earn to make it worthwhile. Diesel was 25p a gallon, a brand new tractor unit, ERF, was £5000 and tyres were £100 each. The costs now have gone ridiculous; I don't know how people make a living.

We used to do three trips a week and at that time the motorway stopped at Lancaster so it was hard work. It was eight or nine hours from here to Glasgow and we had shunters at this end. So the driver would go up, tip, load, drive back, tip and load and the following night go back again. They would come back in on a Saturday morning. Our competitors for the Scottish work were Sid Cope and some of the Scottish firms like W H Malcolms, McCalls and Oswalds Transport who had a depot on the A34.

My dad was a very hard worker. I've never known anyone who could work like him. He would do tiles for Downings and salt for Palmer Mann running to and from London with a Dodge four wheel flat. This was when he was operating from the council house. He'd go and fetch a load of tiles and throw them off on to the garden. Then he'd go to Sandbach and load his salt. So he'd got two loads to deliver but the tiles had got to be delivered first so he'd shovel the salt off on to a sheet on the lawn, put the tiles back on and go and deliver them. Then he'd come back and shovel the salt back on and drive down to London and back. He would never stop. It was the way he was. He achieved a lot through hard work but he couldn't have done it without my mum. She was so supportive; she was his strength, really.

Dad's men were always well paid. They earned their money because of the amount of work they did. In the 1960s and 1970s when the average wage was £10-£15 per week they were earning £70-£80. My dad had a good turnover of drivers because a lot of them couldn't stand the pace. There came a man from Becketts once, a great big fellow. He could tear the world down. I remember when he worked for Becketts he could throw wheels and tyres with the rims and everything in and stack them ten high. The way you had to do it was lay one down and then get the next one and sort of roll it up your leg onto your chest and throw it on top. Well, this guy could stack ten. That's ten truck wheels and tyres. Anyway, he came to my dad and said 'Three trips a week? I'll do five'. He did do the five trips but he only did it twice and then he left. He was absolutely worn out.

Another job dad used to do was bring fire bricks down from G R Steins at Bonnybridge in Scotland. A tremendous amount used to go to South Wales to the steel industry and a lot used to go to the Buxton area (I think it was something to do with limestone) where they needed fire bricks for kilns. He used to fetch these bricks and they'd have an odd pallet here and an odd pallet there that hadn't been delivered because it was out of the way somewhere and they wanted the truck emptied. So occasionally he would pile all this stuff on a trailer and stick a tractor unit on and say *'there you go, deliver that'* when I was old enough to drive. God knows what the weight would be on the trailer - sometimes you'd get on the Buxton Road and not be able to get up the bank and you'd have to reverse back, turn around and go to somewhere like Adams Butter where they'd got forklifts and ask them to take some pallets off.

They were all the same in those days. Sid Cope always ran AEC eight wheelers which were only 24' long so he'd have a load of bricks on the bottom and another load of steel on the top (two loads on one wagon) and these girders were thirty foot long so they stuck out over the edge.

We were based in Bignall End. We started off in Vernon Avenue and then bought a yard at

1 New Road which was a new house and yard and we worked from there until we had about ten vehicles. After that, we rented the old railway station from British Rail. There are houses on that site now. It was a big yard and we ran up to twenty trucks from there.

We had a warehouse which was where the railway trucks had come in so we took the lines up and filled it in and there was a platform, quite a big area. Anyway, we got a job with Minsil's from Northwich, they were cattle food people. They asked us if we could store bone meal for them. Obviously, they would pay us to store it and unload it but there weren't any pallets, it was all on the floor in bags. We had 4000 tons in that building and they'd come some days for as much as 80 tons. It had to be picked up and put on trucks and another day they would send 60 or 70 tons in.

We also ran some wagons on what was then Silcocks, which is now BOCM Pauls, the cattle feed people based in Liverpool. So we had 4 four wheelers and they used to go every morning at 4.00 am to Liverpool and either drop the load in the yard or deliver some of it around the farms in small amounts. It would be nothing for them to work fifteen hours a day, every day. My uncle Ron drove one of them.

We used to do work for Firth Wire Company at Warrington. They did all sorts of wire - coils of wire for springs etc, florist wire which was short lengths in small cardboard boxes, baling wire for paper mills which were great long lengths with a twirl on the end for baling. Dad would put these on with the bricks from Downings. The number of engineering bricks we took to Scotland for the distilleries! They are all built with Staffordshire blue engineering bricks because they aren't porous and they hold temperature. They are solid bricks with no holes in them. When a driver had 6000 bricks on a truck he knew he'd got them on. Anyway, the wire would be put on with the bricks and, of course, the name of game was to get there, get unloaded and back as quickly as possible.

A couple of funny stories come to mind. One of our drivers, Jim Smart, goes to Scotland and he has 6000 'engineers' on for somewhere near Dundee and a ton of baling wire for a Glasgow paper mill. The baling wire is on the top because it's twenty foot long. It's bundled up in small quantities about a hundredweight each and then banded up to about a ton. Now, he's thinking *'I can't get the bricks off until I've got the wire off'* so off he goes early and gets to his Glasgow drop and there's nobody there because they don't start until 8.00 am. The gates are shut but the offices are next door. He sees they have a letter box. So what does he do? He cuts the band wrapped around the wire and feeds the twenty foot pieces through the letterbox. Then he went and delivered the bricks. The people opened the door and they've got a ton of baling wire that's been posted through the letterbox! There was hell up about it - they couldn't get in.

Another time he went down to London with florist wire. Now, florist wire is packed in boxes about 8" x 6" x 2" and it's very heavy. He's got four tons of it to go to this huge florist wholesaler. Anyway, he gets there in the evening and they'd shut up and gone home. Next door is a pub. He goes in *'Excuse me, the people next door - it's all locked up and I've got a delivery for them. I've got a bit of wire for them'*. So the people in the pub say he can leave it there. *'Where do you want me to put it?'* Well, in this pub they've got a piano above the cellar and they say 'Just pop it under the piano'. So he ferries these boxes in and they've got four tons of wire under this piano and the floor was groaning and everything was rolling towards the piano. It never went through the floor though.

We once moved some agricultural steel framed buildings to Scotland and the driver had chained this load on his trailer. Anyway, he drives up the motorway and there was hardly any

An Ernie Owen ERF CI.68. *Arthur Ingram*

A night out at Cottons Hotel. Back L-R: John Belfield, Ernie Owen, ?, David Shipton (Transport Manager Minsal),
?, Spencer Cotton (Mechanic). Middle L-R: Lilian Harding, ?, June Belfield, Frank Phillips (Belfield driver), ?.
Front: ?, ?, June Owen, Rita Phillips, ?. *J Harding Collection*

traffic and just above Lancaster, where some of it was lit, he keeps seeing a flicker in his mirror. It keeps catching his eye and he thinks he'd better pull up and have a look. He pulls on to the hard shoulder and he's got an RSJ 10" deep, 6" wide and 25' long that's come out of the chains. It had shuffled back and slid off the side so it was only in one chain at the back. It was sticking out about 10' to the side. It was lucky he hadn't hit anything.

Our yard was directly opposite a pub called the Plough. Of course, the men used to go in on a Friday night for a pint before they went home. Now with our yard being an old railway station there was a wall alongside where the line was. We had a twenty thousand gallon tank on the wall and it was gravity-feed and you would just pump the diesel in. We never picked fuel up outside; we carried enough fuel for anywhere and back. We used to have the spare wheels on the trailers and a tank both sides - 140 gallons of fuel, 70 each side. The men would come in and put the pipe in the tank and because it was gravity-feed it would take a while. The yard was made up of broken tiles from Downings so you would get a piece of tile and wedge it in the pump handle.

While it was filling you would check the oil, check your lights etc. When that was full you'd chuck the pipe across and fill the tank on the other side. So we were having a drink in the Plough one night and this driver - a little chap from Norton somewhere - comes running across and says *'I forgot about the diesel pump and went to park up. The pipe's ripped off the tank.'* Well, there's about 15000 gallons of fuel in this tank and he's got a rolled up Sentinel stuck in the hole. That's all that was holding it. We went back and it was squirting out everywhere. We ended up knocking a brush stale in overnight and fixing it the next morning. We must have lost 200 gallons of fuel.

I can still remember some of the drivers: Ivan Derricott, Les Sergeant, Phil Darlington, Bill Wild, Jim Smart and Bill Hackney.

Ken Sturge with his 1943 Austin K6. c.1950. The Sturges and the Owens lived two doors from each other in Vernon Avenue and both parked their vehicles there. Ken and Ernie were good friends. *Alan Sturge*

Ian Tyler

I worked for Ernie Owen when I was about 20. He was very nice but you didn't want to get the wrong side of him. He had a vile temper. He chased me round the yard once. I'd got an Atkinson and he'd just done the engine up. Anyway, I was going to Scotland in it and it boiled up just going over Shap. When I got back I told him what had happened. He said *'How much did you put in it?'* Like a fool, I exaggerated and said *'About 8 gallon.'* Anyway, he'd got this watering can in his hand and chased me round the flaming yard trying to hit me with it.

I remember one of the jobs we used to do was collect borax from a place in Belvedere in Kent. Written on the side of the sacks was 'Twenty Mule Train', I think it was American. Anyway, when we got down to this place in Kent these sacks used to come down a conveyor belt and there was a bloke there who used to help you load it. He was only a little bloke and he had a wooden leg. Ernie's trailers weren't the best - there were always holes in them. Well, this bloke used to go mad when he saw us because his wooden leg used to drop in these holes. Then he'd have to manoeuvre to get it out. Sometimes, if it went too deep, he had to unscrew his leg to get it out.

In 1974 I fell asleep at the wheel coming back from Scotland. In those days people did three Scotch a week. I was driving an Atkinson Mk 1 and I was in hospital for 11 months. I sustained severe injuries and was in a plaster cast from my neck to my ankles. I spent the first six months in Lancaster Hospital and the rest at Biddulph Grange.

When I recovered I went back to work but the doctor had told me to do only light work. Well, Ernie immediately gave me a a load of wire for Scotland with five drops, all hand-ball, so I decided it was time to leave and I got a job with Chapman and Ball.

A poor photo - but it gives an idea of what was left of the Atkinson.

Right: Ian in traction at Lancaster Infirmary after his accident, prior to his operation to pin and put him in plaster from shoulder to foot. He is being attended to by Nurse Betty Addison. He was later transferred from Lancaster to Biddulph Grange.

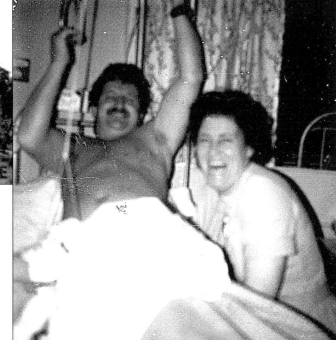

JOHN T HEATHCOTE LIMITED: John Heathcote

I bought my first trucks, a Bedford TK and a Ford, in April 1962. I was already married to Hilda at this time and we set up the business together. We operated from a site at Greenbank Road, Tunstall which I'd bought from my father. The Ford was a coal-bagging truck but they both had a 50 mile radius licence. Licences in those days were required to run vehicles - a C licence was for manufacturers to carry their own goods, a B licence was a limited licence for general goods with a radius of 25 miles or 50 miles and an A licence was the one we all wanted which allowed you to travel all over the country. The TK was working for T W Beckett of Fenton delivering coal from Wolstanton Colliery to the Gas Works at Cannock and Shrewsbury. A day's work might consist of a load to Cannock and one to Shrewsbury. I also started to take on work for Downings, British Salt and was carrying foundry sand for a firm in Willenhall.

After about six months I bought two vehicles from Meadowcroft Brothers of Kidsgrove and then a Bedford TK from J Ray and Sons at Chell. After that I acquired more licences until I had 17 vehicles altogether. I wanted the licenses; I wanted to get on to distance work as fast as possible. After I bought vehicles I would modernise them so I could get the tonnage on. I remember I bought my first A licence from Richard Oridge (known as Dickie Richmond) in 1966.

Obviously, when I first started out I was doing the driving myself and Hilda got the work. She would ring Downings to find out where my next load was and when I rang in to say I was on the way back she'd tell me where to get the return load. If I was doing maintenance on a truck and wanted spares she'd jump in her car and go to Atkinsons at Preston to fetch them.

I can remember in 1964 when I bought a tanker from Whalebourne Motors. I'd been to Dagenham and saw this eight wheel tanker for sale - it was priced at £400 and had a Gardner engine in. I wanted the vehicle but I didn't want the tank. Anyway, I bought the truck for £350 and they agreed to take it to their Chelford depot where they told me I could take the tank off myself. Norman Cadwalder was working for me at the time so he dropped me off at Chelford and after I'd taken the tank off he came back and we towed it back to Stoke. Norman Beech of Beechs Garage put a flat body on it and it went on the road. Norman Beech was a great bloke. You could talk to him. He sprayed a vehicle for me once and I was under the impression it was included in the price of the truck and he said it wasn't. When I said I didn't want to pay he said 'I'll tell you what, I'll meet you half way'. That was the sort of man he was - I paid half and he paid half.

I had a vehicle wrote off in about 1966/67. We had a load of salt to be delivered from ICI to Basingstoke Council and the driver who was supposed to take it down couldn't do it. Anyway, I took it and I was driving this eight wheeler on the Basingstoke by-pass near Guildford at about 1.30 in the morning when an estate car came along on my side of the road and hit me. The driver was killed. It was in the early hours of the morning but there were two witnesses - a petrol pump attendant and a milkman - who had seen what had happened and testified that the driver of the car had caused it. My vehicle was replaced by the first articulated vehicle in the Potteries. Norman Beech supplied it. He supplied them all; I spent a fortune with him.

I managed to buy all these trucks because I ploughed the profits I made back into the business. I was always looking for an opportunity to get into the big firms. I always paid my drivers by the job not by the hour. I would say to them 'Look, lads, if you're not making money, I'm not making money'. On Saturdays, after washing wagons off I would take the lads over to the British Legion for a pint and hear all about what was going on elsewhere. By 1967 I'd outgrown the premises and had to find another yard. The council offered me the railway goods yard in Tunstall. They wanted me to buy it but I couldn't afford it at the time. I converted a building into a warehouse where I used to store the loads . I had two forklifts - one a Hyster 7.5 tonner for lifting containers on and off and the other a 2.5 ton Coventry Climax, for normal work. Forklifts came in in about 1962/63 I think.

In 1968 I started carrying generators for British Railways. They contacted me through a chap named Arnold Coynes who was the Road Haulage Association negotiator. He was a very nice man and he put my name forward to the workshops in Crewe. They paid me £100 up and £100 back which was a lot of money in those days. That was up to Glasgow. Mind you, it was a day to load, a night to go up and a day to reload and down again. They took the old generator off and put a new one on so you were loaded both ways.

I also carried machinery for a big fabricating firm which made boilers and things like that. There was an incident when I was carrying a boiler destined for Croydon. It was 12ft wide and 16 ft high - I remember it would only just go under the motorway bridges. Anyway, I'd notified the police in London who were, incidentally, Scotland Yard, that the load would be on its way down so they could escort it. Apparently, the customer had someone in a car going down with this boiler and when it got to St Albans they had it diverted to Harlow. This was without my knowledge. At about 11.00 am I get a call from Scotland Yard *'Where's this load?'* They'd had a policeman on a motorbike waiting for it since 9.00 am. It was only when I contacted the customer that I found out what had happened. The police were going to throw the book at me and I didn't know anything about it.

I used to do work for ERF taking cabs up to Blackpool where they fitted out the interiors. I'd take a load up and bring one back. I also worked for Gardner engines - I have a letter they sent to me and a photograph of the biggest load to come out of their factory.

I can remember one occasion when we had to take a couple of loads of bricks down to Bury St Edmunds. I was driving one truck and Norman was driving the other. We started off at 8.00 at night and arrived there at about 2.30 in the morning. I'd only got about 2000 bricks on so I suggested we offload them first so I could get away because I'd got 6 tons of salt to deliver to the East End of London. We were planning to meet up in Thurrock. So we backed on to this building site to where we thought they'd want the bricks and started to offload them when suddenly we're surrounded by coppers. The Sergeant says *'Aah, Gotcha!'* I said *'What do you mean, Gotcha?'* He wanted to know what we were doing and I showed him the conveyance note. I said to him *'You don't think we've come down from Stoke to pinch bricks, do you?'* He later told us that the Chief Constable had bought one of these houses which was why all these coppers had arrived. He said *'Oh, he's going to have a red face in the morning'*.

I also remember when one of my trucks went through London to Ramsgate for flints. On the way back the driver didn't notice that they'd changed the road into a one-way system and he got stopped by the police. Anyway, he'd had a pint or two in Ramsgate and he was over the limit. They took him to the police station but they left the vehicle on the road. Now, it was a vehicle with air brakes and they won't go when the air is used up and when they tried to drive it away it wouldn't go. They rang me in the middle of the night and said *'Your driver has immobilized the vehicle'*. They couldn't get it to go because they weren't building the air pressure up in the tank. Anyway, in the end, I had to go down to London to get the vehicle off the road and bring it home. He was one of the first people to be done for drinking and driving.

We'd got a four wheeler with a specially built 22ft body which carried clay from Websters,

Tunstall to Fulham Pottery. It was also used for delivering cartons to London Airport every other night for Stafford Crown Pottery and crockery from Dunn and Bennetts in Burslem to all the hotels in London. These had to be night time deliveries as it was too busy in the day to unload them. If I'd got a Heinz delivery to NW10 of 20 tons of salt, I'd put the crockery cartons on top as there was no real weight in them. They'd be offloaded straight on to the aircraft. I'd be getting £5 a carton in those days - this was the 'cream' on the load for us.

At the peak of our business we had 17 wagons and extra trailers which were used for loading. We had drivers for every wagon and shunters who loaded the trailers and brought them to the depot. We also had our own mechanics.

In about 1969 one of Belfield's drivers, Ryan Tarrant, was killed when his truck was involved in an accident. I and several other owners and managers decided to hold a dance at the Queen's Hall in Burslem to raise money for his eight children. He was a popular man and the dance was a huge success raising about £1200. Our accountant put the money into a Building Society so they could all have a share when they reached 21. That's what haulage was like in those days, we helped each other.(See Belfields)

We were by now living in Sandbach. In about 1970 we moved from the station yard to the Cafe and Garage at Talke, opposite the Caldwell Arms. It was the old Shell garage. Anyway, in 1972 Vic Wild bought the lot off me - he offered me a good price and I accepted. However, I couldn't leave transport alone and set up again six months later as HTC but operated from Twemlow Green so we could be nearer home.

In about 1976 we went to Spain for a holiday as we were in much need of a break. Our son, Derek, looked after the business while we were away. I was diagnosed with a serious illness; the doctors told me that I could be dead in six months if I continued the way I was. We'd bought this place in Anglesey and we decided to sell up and move here. Do I miss it? Yes, I do but money isn't everything. Transport is in our blood and we always think and talk about it. Hilda was my business partner, my wife and friend. We worked as a team along with our sons. We were able to give our sons a good education. David came into the business after college and Derek went to ERFs as an apprentice and later travelled all over the world as an engineer.

I'm still a hard worker even though I am 84. I'd like to think that people remember that my trucks were never empty. Everyone who knows me in transport knows that I've never asked a man to do something I couldn't do myself.

Hilda and John Heathcote celebrating their silver wedding anniversary in 1974.

A line-up of Heathcote lorries at Station Yard, Tunstall c.1969 - shown across 2 pages.

John Heathcote with the largest load of Gardner engines to come out of the factory at Barton Hall Engine Works, Eccles, Manchester, May 1976.

This ERF was built specially for J T Heathcote.
It was used for carrying cartons of crockery to the hotels in London and to the airport for Air Canada, c.1968.

One of the generators for British Rail photographed at Station Yard, Tunstall.

Photos J and H Heathcote collection

A Road Haulage Society Dinner Dance. Front: Harold Dunne (Manager Beech's) with Joan Dunne opposite.
Middle: Eric Latham (Manager British Salt) with Hilda Latham opposite.
Back: John Heathcote with Hilda opposite.

THE WILD GROUP - VIC WILD:

Derek Hambleton

Vic Wild, also known as 'The Vicar' or 'The Wild Man', started in the road haulage business with an ex-BRS eight wheeler on de-nationalization in about 1953. At this time he was landlord of the newly opened Apedale Hotel at Knutton, Newcastle which he ran with his first wife, Nan. He also owned and drove a taxi. When the eight-wheeler was purchased he gave up the taxi and started driving the lorry but still did a share of the pub work. Some time later he entered into partnership with Frank Condon and formed Wild-Condon Limited, running a fleet of mainly eight wheelers carrying roof tiles and also tyres from the Dunlop factory in Stoke. Dunlop, incidentally, manufactured the model whale for the film 'Moby Dick' which was transported to Elstree Studios on a Wild-Condon eight-wheeler.

Derek Hambleton who worked for Vic Wild in the 1960s and 70s.

The partnership with Frank Condon was dissolved after a slight altercation which culminated in Vic deciding that Frank's office would be a good place to store tarpaulins, ropes and spare wheels and he proceeded to fill it up with these items while Frank, who was a 'natty' dresser, was still in there. Frank left and later went on to form Metallic Roadways which had offices in Stoke and also in the St Albans area.

In the photograph of the Wild-Condon fleet, the first vehicle to be painted in the familiar two-tone blue with white stripe livery, registration number SVT 646, can be seen bringing up the rear.

Wild Condon Fleet lined up on the A34 at Trentham, 1950s. *G Pritchard Collection*

An interesting story concerning this period of the company's history is that a contract was taken on to transport bulk sulphur. The problem was that this had to be done on tipping vehicles and at this time Vic only owned one tipper. This was overcome by loading sided wagons with the sulphur and then shovelling it onto a tipper near to the delivery point. Obviously, this was a very dangerous and dusty job and no safety equipment in the form of headgear or goggles was provided.

Over the next few years, Vic proceeded to expand with the acquisition of Gleave Transport of Audlem, James Frost Transport of Wolstanton, Lloyds Transport of Trafford Park, North Shropshire Transport of Gobowen near Oswestry, W J Tancock Transport of Exeter and Madden Transport of Cambourne, Cornwall. He also made a foray into quarry machinery manufacture; the company was called Wild-Simpson Limited. Vibrating screens were made to grade and separate materials but the business was short-lived as the screens had a tendency to self-destruct. This was probably due to the fact that some of their components were obtained by breaking up old pianos.

When I joined the company in 1968 as an office junior, it was a real family affair with Vic's brother, Frank, running the traffic office, another brother Edgar and a nephew, Chris, working in accounts and one of Vic's sisters, Audrey, doing the typing. The fleet at this time was a mixture of ERF, Atkinson, Foden and Seddon trucks, all Gardner engines - Vic's lorries were all roughly the same: Gardner engine, David Brown gearbox and Kirkstall axles. Many of the trucks were conversions of one sort or another ie eight-wheelers cut down to make two or three axle trailer units. The Fodens had most of their original components replaced to make them as close as possible in spec to the other makes.

This ERF was the oldest vehicle Vic had when Derek was there - it was based permanently at Gimsons in the 1960s. George Pritchard used to drive the Taylor Grab. *G Pritchard Collection*

The oldest vehicle then was a 1937 ERF, registration number CTF 837. The newest vehicles were 1968 ERF and Atkinson tractor units. CTF 837 was based at Gimson Refractories in Fenton and most nights three trailers loaded with HVAR clay would come up from Exeter on night trunk for Gimsons. It all had to be unloaded with shovels and Vic would often go up there to help shovel the clay off. He would drive up in his Mark Ten Jaguar, usually dressed in a nice suit, a pair of yellow 'dealer' boots and a woolly hat. He sometimes went up there in a bad mood and often caused complaints as he would be none too careful where the clay landed when it left his shovel. This once resulted in a toe-to-toe argument with a pottery manager which very nearly ended in a fight. In the early 1970s Vic decided that he would have no more loose clay in his lorries and all the side-boards were removed from the trailers, piled up and burned.

Vic liked his vehicles to be kept clean, inside and out. He would often be seen washing off trailers. Drivers were responsible for their own tractor units which had to be washed a minimum of once a week. If Vic opened the cab door and he saw it was dirty inside it would sometimes result in him soaking the inside of the cab and the contents with disinfectant. He also liked the trucks to be well maintained and there were usually around eight mechanics employed along with a body-builder and a coach painter.

A fault which happened from time to time with Gardner engines was that an exhaust valve would fail and break off causing the engine to 'knock'. This once happened to a vehicle that was driven by a man who always had a black dog with him called Prince. The driver was in the Traffic Office telling the tale of what had happened. He said that he saw Prince's ears prick up just before the knock started, so the dog had heard the fault before he had. Vic said that the best thing to do was sack the driver and set the dog on in his place.

Actually, very few employees were ever dismissed. Drivers used to drift away to other firms and then come back again; it was just accepted as the normal course of events.

During the 1970s other companies were purchased including Towells Haulage of Stamford, Lincs; McPhee Transport of Newcastle upon Tyne and Wolverhampton and Hugh Clelland Transport of Chryston near Glasgow - which was renamed Wild (Scotland) Limited.

When new companies were taken over normally the size of their fleets would be reduced and vehicles surplus to requirements would be sold off. These vehicles would usually be the rigids and the newer 'high value' vehicles that did not come up to Vic's approved spec. For example, when McPhees was acquired their fleet included 14 Scania 110 tractor units; they were the newest vehicles they had and were engaged in a double-shifted 'trunk' operation between Newcastle Upon Tyne and Wolverhampton. They each completed 14 trips each week covering about 6000 miles in the process. These vehicles were immediately sold to bring back capital and the work they did was covered by the general haulage fleet and a down-sized trunk operation.

Wild (Scotland) Limited fared rather better in as much as their F86 Volvos were retained until they were replaced with new MAN and Mercedes vehicles.

Another small company taken over in the 1970s was Swales Transport of Hartlepool which ran a fleet of 4 AEC Mandator tractor units. Vic's pet hate was AECs; he often said they should be prosecuted for making them. These vehicles were put into service at Stoke depot, doing a night trunk to Hartlepool and then used as shunters on day shift. The order from Vic was to run them until the first one broke down and then to cannibalise it to keep the others running until they were all 'dead'. This took about six weeks; Vic was right about AECs.

I mentioned before that Wild (Scotland) Limited's vehicles were replaced with new MAN and Mercedes vehicles. There had been a shift in policy in 1973 as to which vehicles were bought. The demise of British manufactured trucks, as far as Vic was concerned, came about when Gardner Engines went on strike. Of course, this caused a shortage of engines and spare parts and when the new 8LXB Gardner engine was introduced only three tractor units were delivered before supplies dried up. These were all Atkinsons although 1 ERF was delivered but it was sent back to the supplier. The new design had the engine protruding from the back of the cab and ERF had decided to cover this with something that Vic thought looked like a chicken shed that 'belonged in a farmyard', hence its return.

Vic Wild
J Longshaw

Gardners was also ensuring that fleets that hadn't traditionally run their engines were getting supplied in an effort to drum up new business. This didn't go down well with Vic. Something had to be done about replacing vehicles and as luck would have it a representative from a DAF agency called. After a demonstration, three DAF 2600s were ordered. These trucks proved to be very successful and once the foreign manufacturers had their foot in the door it was goodbye to Gardners.

During the 1970s the 'bread and butter' traffic was mainly flat and coiled steel - ten British Steel factories were serviced by the fleet. Tyres, bricks, salt, concrete pipes, cider and timber were also carried in large quantities along with yet more steel from a variety of privately owned factories and steel stockholders. In those days when the drivers arrived at Taunton Cider they were allowed to quench their thirst from a drum kept there for the purpose! In winter large quantities of fish were carried from the West Country to Belgium in refrigerated trailers.

In the spring, cauliflower and new potatoes were carried from Brittany to all parts of the UK, mainly coming in through Plymouth on unaccompanied trailers which had previously been sent out to France 'piggy-backed'. Often they were for a timed delivery; sometimes they were expected at Glasgow or Edinburgh markets five or six hours after clearing customs. The MAN and Mercedes trucks were fast but there are limits; delivery times often needed to be re-arranged which usually entailed someone having to ring the delivery points at 10 or 11 o clock in the evening as the fruit and vegetable merchants were only open through the night. I can remember one particular incident involving a load of cauliflowers. When the driver arrived at Redmans in Middlesborough, there was nobody there so he unloaded and stacked the load by a roller-shutter door. When the man opening the warehouse that night pulled the door up he triggered an avalanche of crates and cauliflowers. The customer wasn't happy.

Some of the staff I remember particularly well was the Taylor family. John 'Geordie' Taylor, his son, John, and a cousin, Barry Nicholson, were all drivers at Wilds. They were later joined by another of Geordie's sons, Ray Taylor. All of these originated in the Esh Winning area of Co. Durham and had moved to Stoke having previously been employed in coal mining. John Taylor junior's sons, David and Chad, carry on the family's tradition of HGV driving up to the present day.

Vic was also involved in warehousing and owned sites at Exeter, Cullompton and Taunton. The site at Cullompton was acquired along with Whittons Transport, another 1970s acquisition. The Warehouses were mainly used to store fertilizer and soap products for ICI and Lever Brothers respectively. Milk powder, part of the infamous Common Market 'mountain' was also stored.

The 'Owner Driver' Scheme:

In the early 1970s Vic introduced a scheme in which drivers were given help in obtaining an Operator's Licence. They then hired a vehicle from the company and basically ran their own business. All the work they did was done through the company on a clearing house basis using a self billing invoice system. Many of the Stoke drivers got involved in this after drivers from Leeds, Nottingham and Carlisle were taken on on this basis, although few were successful in the long run.

In the 1970s Vic became involved in the Hotel industry - his first acquisition was the Durose Transport Cafe and Hotel on the A34 at Cross Heath, Newcastle. This property was completely gutted and refurbished and then re-opened as The Ambassador Motel. It was then sold to Bass Breweries and Vic took The Borough Arms at Newcastle as part-exchange. This was followed by a string of other hotels and pubs. I have not mentioned until now Vic's second wife, Barbara, who became involved in the running of this branch of the empire. She also ran a dog boarding kennel at their home at Rough Close and bred and showed pedigree Pekinese dogs.

The end of the transport operations by The Wild Group came in the 1981/82 period when the fleet was gradually sold. I think that Vic was ready to retire from full time work - he was usually at work seven days a week. The Hotel side of the business continued but this too was gradually reduced and sold off. Vic died in 1988.

Gordon Bloor

When you worked for Vic he wanted his pound of flesh, like they all did. The problem I'd got wasn't with Vic himself, it was the work. It was either hand-ball or shovel off or shovel on - it was damned hard work.

One of my memories of Vic was in about 1958, when they used to have the old licences. He had bought this company called Maddens Transport in Cambourne. Apparently, if you bought a company in another area you could only employ people who lived there. Vic came out to me one day and said *'I'm changing you to this other truck - if anybody stops you tell them you live in Truro'* Anyway, I'm stopped by this copper and I told him I lived in Truro and I could see it in his face that he knew I was lying. He said *'Whereabouts?'* I had to give a fictitious address and started to walk away when he says *'In a minute, Driver, can I have a word with you?'* I went round the back of the wagon and he says, *'There's no such place.'* I said, *'I know; I've just made it up.'* Then we both burst out laughing and I went on my way.

I left Vic and went to work for Sid Cope up the top of Hartshill. He had a very small yard but he got all his trucks in - he had about ten, I think. He ran AECs with high cabs - they called them 'Park Royal' cabs. We were loading girders off Shelton Bar with these AEC eight wheelers. These girders were too long for the vehicle so there was an overhang at the back and at the front.

We also carried flat steel that was used for something in the building industry. With this you'd have to stop every so often to try to push the load up because it kept slipping I remember we used to go to a cafe at Worcester that was open all night. There were always blokes with containers, old fashioned ones, or a box van or something parked up there and you'd back up to them and push these sheets back up again. Then you'd set off and the same thing would happen again.

We'd be working 16 hours at least. In about 1960/62 Sid Cope was paying £8 a trip to Cornwall and you did three trips one week and two the next.

George Pritchard

I worked for Vic from about 1965 to 1971. It wasn't continuous; I went to work for Beresfords for a while and then went back. I remember I rode down to the yard on my bike when I was fifteen and

Straight out of the paint shop! 1974/5. *D Hambleton Collection*

Lloyds Transport of Trafford Park was taken over by Vic.
In this picture, taken at the yard in Whieldon Road are L-R: Cliff Weaver, Jack Gore and 'Yogi Bear' (real name
George Fenwick). The man inside the cab 'waving' is Jimmy Jameson. 888 KVT was a cut-down 8 wheeler.

One of North Shropshire's ERFs. This was an export model for Turkey but got smashed up en route so was returned to ERF. Vic bought it and put the 2nd steer on. There was a manual splitter on the right side of the driver. One of the drivers of this was Alfie Taylor.

A Tancocks loaded with hay tedders - the man just out of shot is Cyril Hughes.

Vic standing in front of one of Lloyds. This was the first day out for this lorry - it became Yogi's rig.

J Frost Transport of Wolstanton was another acquisition - this is taken at Frost's depot.

BELOW:
A Gleave Transport Atki with a Massey Ferguson load. The driver was Cyril Hughes.

BELOW:
One of the screens that Vic's company Wild-Simpson manufactured, being pulled by CBV 747, max speed 25mph. Later converted into a tipper and used for the red ash job at Parkhouse.

asked for a job and he gave me one 'for my cheek'. My wage was £2 15s but I got a rise when the lady who worked at the printers across the way asked me how much Vic was paying me. When I told her she said she'd have a word with him and he put my money up to £5 10s. My dad worked for him as well. His name was George but everyone knew him as Pedro. He'd worked for Bartlams and for Daveys at one time; he drove 77 JVT which was one of their eight wheelers.

George Pritchard Sr (Pedro) by his ERF loaded with coils of steel, late 1960s.

I remember I was with my dad one night on one of the services and we saw one of Ernie Owens - they used to run through the night to avoid the ministry - and my dad said, *'Just look at that trailer.'* This driver was carrying three loads: a load of flat steel first then a load of tiles on top and a load of salt on top of that and the trailer was bowed in the middle.

One of the blokes who worked for Vic was Alfie Taylor and he told me a story about when he worked on BRS. There were three of them in Scotland and one of the men died in his cab. They'd gone to his lorry in the morning and couldn't wake him and realised he was dead. Anyway, because they knew what a hassle it was going to be to get the body back they just tied him in the passenger seat with a rope and brought him back. This was in the late 1950s and it would have taken six or eight hours to get back. They took him home to his widow. 'Here's your husband, I'm afraid he's dead'. When he was telling the story he couldn't stop laughing. The authorities went mad.

I've always enjoyed drawing and painting and in 1979 Ron Dale bought a Seddon Atkinson from Rylands, the Atkinson agent in Tunstall and asked me to design the livery for it. When I'd done this and they'd had it painted Ron told me that Atkinsons were making a promotional record 'Riding the Big A' and wanted a picture for the album's sleeve. He asked me to take the lorry to a photo shoot they were doing at Hem Heath Colliery and the Woodley Cafe at Barlaston. There were four vehicles there: one of Beresfords, one of Rogers from Leek and one of Walchesters and we spent a few hours having our pictures taken. When we'd finished they took us for a meal at the Post House at Clayton.

A young George Pritchard jr. taken at Whieldon Road depot c.1968.

Kenny Seratt

Ridin' the big A

From the sleeve to the album 'Riding the Big A' which shows the Dale lorry with George Jr driving.
Ray Condliffe was driving Walchester's. The driver of the Roger's vehicle is unknown.
To the left (not shown here) is a Beresford vehicle which was driven by Kane Mayer.

OPPOSITE PAGE:
Painted by George Pritchard Jr. It shows his dad at the front with Harry Barnett, in Ward Street, Hanley,
which has now been demolished. The lorry is one of Sid Cope's, AUS 53S.

G Pritchard Collection

W SMITH HAULAGE: Don Smith

My father, William Smith, was born on May 11 1906. His father kept the Dolphin Inn in Cobridge Road, Hanley. Father was 15 when he set up in business with a Model T Ford taxi in 1922.

He bought his first lorry, a Morris Commercial 2 tonner, in 1926 during the coal strike of that year. It had double wheels on the rear so he could put 4 tons on, and he was basically transporting coal and pottery locally. His business thrived and he built Bedford House and Bedford Garage (so called because he always ran Bedfords) in Bromley Street, Hanley in about 1930. To the rear of the house was the transport yard.

During the war years he had some of his vehicles requisitioned by the MOD - some were transporting pebbles from the beach at Seatown in Dorset to Dunkerswell Aerodrome where they were used to make the runways for Spitfires.

Father had about 28 lorries when road transport was nationalized. Nationalization was short-lived and he was able to put vehicles on the road again in1952 with contract licences to the sandpit he owned at Hassell Green, Alsager. He had three of his old drivers working for him on this job - Wilf Morris, Billy Robinson and George Wyms. A lot of builders were buying sand from him and this is how he managed to build up a large portfolio of property in the Potteries. When some of these builders got into financial difficulty, he would take a property as payment.

Father also owned a red ash mound in Clough Street, Hanley. He sold and transported this ash to Manchester where it was used to build the airport. He started on this in about 1954/5 and was still operating it in 1964 when he died. I think it finished in about 1968.

When he died he had a fleet of 40 vehicles. When I took over I built the business up to 68 lorries. It was mainly long-distance work down to Dorset, Devon and Cornwall. I ran ERFs, Albions and Leylands - artics, tippers and artics with tipping bodies. John Jenks and Vic Wild were running to the same areas as us.

I sold part of the business in 1970 to Patten and Heap and carried on running about 6 vehicles until 5 years ago when I bought DWP out. These were Scania lorries with fridge boxes travelling to France and Belgium bringing back foodstuffs, and working as W Smith (Stoke on Trent) Ltd.

When I was seventy I decided to retire. I concentrate now on my collection of vintage lorries which I take to all the shows.

A W. Smith 1966 Commer tipper with a Commer two stroke engine. Wilf Morris drove this. c. 1966.

An impressive line-up of Bedford vehicles at the depot at
Bedford Garage, Bromley Street, Hanley. 1931

ABOVE:
Three times a week a
Smith vehicle would take
10 tons of salt to
Glastonbury. This picture
was in the local paper
under the heading 'Stop
and look again' as the
road system had been
changed to a one-way.
The driver was Freddie
Brooks. c.1968.

LEFT:
This was one of two
Seddons supplied by
Bailey's Garage on Leek
Road, Hanley to W
Smith. 1947.

ABOVE:
John Jenks offered
Don the job of taking
Turner's asbestos to
Devon and Cornwall
in the 1970s as John
didn't have any four-
wheelers to do it.

*All photos D Smith
Collection*

One of Don's vintage vehicles. New in 1936, it once
belonged to Chipperfield's Circus. Don remembers
seeing a picture of it carrying two cages with a lion
in each. He bought it about four years ago.

RIGHT:
Eddie Timmins drove this when it was new. It first
went on the road on 1st April 1966. Don bought it
in 2007. Picture taken at Betley Show.

J WARBURTON & SONS: Dave Warburton

My grandfather, James Warburton, was an engineer for Rolls Royce working on plane engines during the war. He started the haulage business in about 1946 transporting coal.

When British Road Services took over all the transport operations they gave my grandad some work on Daniel Platts - not many people wanted this work as it was all hand-ball. Daniel Platts made quarry tiles. Grandad used to take the tiles to Liverpool docks and bring fruit back for the fruit merchants in Stoke. As soon as my dad Jimmy and his brother could drive they were in a truck. Up until the early 1970s there was just my grandad, my dad and Uncle George - three trucks, all flatbeds doing the same type of work

At Platts the tiles would be loaded loose; it was a finger-shredding job because they were sharp. I can remember when we would back the flat beds into a bay and it would take a good day to load them. The bay was sunk into the floor and they would bring the tiles to the side of the truck

James Warburton Sr.
Taken at Kays Trucks office (now Imperial Commercials, Cobridge), 20 Sept. 1983.

by forklift but even then they would still be taken off the pallets and loaded by hand. This was probably in the late 1960s. There was a gang of Platts' men who would load them perfectly - the tiles weren't roped and sheeted as such, there would just be a rope around the back end . Nothing ever came off. My father helped with the loading as well. Nowadays, drivers just shut the curtains and go to sleep but in those days you helped. It was hard work. Even when Platts got a bit more modern and loaded the trucks with forklifts and pallets, you'd get to the destination and if there wasn't a forklift you'd still have to do it by hand.

There were two parts to the Platts factory - one part was where they did the clay tiles and the other was where they made the dust-dressed tiles. These tiles looked the same but were made differently. They had this big hopper where the dust was compressed with a bit of moisture into a tile. They were packed in cartons so could be banded on pallets and loaded with a forklift but mostly we did the loose tiles. When we went on to artics we could just drop a trailer in the bay for them and take the one they'd loaded the day before. With the little rigids it was perhaps half a day to load and when you got to where you were going it was as many hours as it took depending on how many men were doing it. I can remember going with my dad and it used to be five or six hours to unload with a gang of men. We worked for Platts until they went into administration five years ago.

I can remember being down Platts one day with my dad. I was driving the forklift and lost control and went into this pit. I'd only be about five or six. No Health and Safety in those days. I drove anything. I drove my father's Volkswagen beetle on a campsite in Dorset when I was about seven and I can remember driving my first artic when I was twelve. I was on Platts and I was in this truck with my dad sitting beside me. I knew how to start it up and how to put it in gear but I'd never driven it. Anyway, he said *'Right, press your clutch, put it in gear, handbrake off, away you go'*. It was all on tickover and I drove out of this bay. As soon as the cab came out of the building my dad jumped out and walked round the front and told me where to drive it. It was a big steering wheel; there was no power steering in those days, I had to stand to operate it.

For a while in the late 70s we did a bit of continental work - two loads a week to Brussels but the competition chopped the rates so we didn't bother any more.

In the early days our vehicles were mainly Leyland Comets; I can remember my dad saying he had an old beaver-nosed comet that he wouldn't let anyone else drive because it was so fast. He was a bit of a speed freak. My granddad had an old Sentinel. He had a crash going along Dock Road in Liverpool in the 1950s. It was a miracle he got out; there was nothing left of the cab. Apparently, he fell out of it and when the police arrived he was standing by the vehicle having one of his Park Drives. He always used to smoke them right down to the end. Even when the new fags came out that had filters on he'd set fire to them to get rid of the filters.

There used to be such a lot of characters about. It was good fun. Jim Stubbs worked for us,

he was a character. Dave Scarlett's another. I called somewhere in Scotland and saw a couple of Beresford trucks and went in. Then I hear this loud voice 'Here's Warbo', it was Dave. Anyway, a bit later on when he went to the toilet we put a couple of tables up against the door. When he opened the door '*What the... hell is going on here*' the next thing there are tables everywhere. Just a night out.

George Warburton (left) with brother Jim outside the pub at the bottom of Hot Lane, Burslem. Early 1960s.

Jim Warburton driving a Seddon at their first depot in Bursley Road, Cobridge.

James Warburton, May 1978
outside the garage in Stonor
Street, Cobridge with a
Seddon Atkinson KVT 605P.

Two Warburton vehicles: a Seddon
and a Leyland Comet. Early 1960s.
Taken at Bursley Road depot.

All Photos D Warburton Collection

BELOW:
Atkinson Borderer OLM 927L
loaded with tiles at Daniel Platts,
Tunstall.

A & H DAVEY (ROADWAYS) LIMITED: Barry Davey

My grandfather came to Stoke from Southern England in about 1936. My father, Arthur Davey, was one of four sons; three of them went into the forces but when my father went to enlist he was turned down. He was left at home to run the family haulage business, A E Davey & Sons. They had a yard in Albert Street, Newcastle from where they did general haulage work but flint from Shoreham for the pottery industry was always the return load.

When the war ended my three uncles came home and expected good jobs in the business but my father had been running it successfully for several years so he decided it was time to leave. After working for a time for Charlie Durose and Basford Garage (both hauliers) he thought he'd get his own wagon. In 1944/45 he sold his Wolsley car (registration number EVT 32) and he and my mother, Hilda, bought their first vehicle, a Morris Commercial. As he didn't have a car any more he bought a push bike to get around on.

The new company was called A & H Davey Transport Limited and it was based in James Street, Wolstanton. They gradually built up to five vehicles: a Maudesley eight wheeler; an ERF six wheeler 'chinese' twin steer; 2 four wheel ERFs and a Thorneycroft. At nationalization the company was taken over by BRS and my father ran it for them for a while. However, he decided that he wanted to be his own boss again and bought two coaches.

In the beginning these coaches were running to places like Blackpool Illuminations and Chatsworth; Dad would be driving one coach and John Heathcote the other. Hilda, John's wife, would go along as well. They also did work for a firm called Globe Tours. In the spring of 1951 they were taking people from the Potteries down to the Festival of Britain exhibition in London. They would leave Stoke at midnight, travel down the A5 (no motorways in those days) to Regents Park and come back the next night. During the three weeks of the holiday period they did trips for Fields End Coaches in Manchester taking people to Blackpool. The pick-up would be at Rigby Road, near the football ground. Sometimes, when they got back from there, they would do a trip to New Brighton and back. Dad also started doing tours to Spain and Portugal - few people would have dreamt of going there at that time.

John and Hilda Heathcote pose beside 'Barry' and 'Kathleen', the two coaches purchased by Arthur after nationalization. *Photo J & H Heathcote*

At de-nationalization my father was one of the first in the area to take the opportunity to get back into long distance haulage. He and my mother were photographed being presented with the log books to 5 six-ton Thorneycrofts they'd successfully tendered for from BRS.

When I left school my father wanted me to have an apprenticeship at Fodens at Elworth. I remember the first day very well - I caught the 4.20 miners' bus to Burslem, changed buses to

Arthur and Hilda Davey being presented with the log books to 5 six-ton Thorneycrofts they had tendered for.

Front L-R: Mr Calderbank, BRS; Hilda and Arthur Davey.

Back L-R: Dennis Cowen, ?, ?, ?, Eric Morley, ?.

Sandbach and got another to Elworth. I also had to attend night school and I remember I had to catch the bus home, then cycle to night school and cycle home again. Of course, after that I had homework to do and had to be up early to catch the 4.20 am bus next morning. I was often late on the night school days - I was dependent on the buses running on time. In the end, it was quicker to hitch-hike.

This went on for some time. My father, being the way he was, thought he'd give me a 'basinful' of this but eventually said *'Right, I've decided I'm going to pay for 10 driving lessons and if you pass first time, I'll buy you a car'*. I knew I'd got to pass this test. I'll never forget it, I was tested on the Saturday when Stoke were playing Hull in the Cup; this would be about 1953, and I passed. My father was as good as his word and bought me a Standard Eight. It's the only car number I remember, TVT 287. He'd said to me *'There's your car, now you've got to run it'* and I was only on £1 something a week as an apprentice. So, I'd got a car to go to work in and there were one or two people that I used to give a lift to which helped with the petrol.

At weekends I used to do some manual work with him, shovelling flint off on a Saturday and Sunday morning - I used to get 2s 6d for that. He'd give me 10s for working all weekend with him.

My parents went to Jersey on holiday in 1955 - my father loved it there and wanted Kathleen (my sister) and I to see it so he paid for us to go the following year. My sister's birthday was on August 1st and the following day it was the Battle of Flowers. I'll never forget it. We went to see this and when we got back to the hotel the manager said *'I want you to ring home'*. My father had come home for lunch and had died. He was 44.

One minute I was working at Fodens and the next I was running this business. I was just 20. My mother got in touch with the local MP because if I wasn't working at Fodens doing the apprenticeship then I should have gone into the forces to do National Service. As it happened, National Service was coming to an end and I didn't have to do it.

I was plunged straight in at the deep end with the business. All I'd done was labouring for father so I didn't know very much about it. My sister had worked for him doing the accounts but it was a matter of learning as we went along. Bassetts were very good to me. Father and Reg Bassett were good friends and Reg rang up and said *'If I can help in any way I will'*. I said that I hadn't got a clue about wages and the men had to be paid so I asked him if he could show me how to do the PAYE. He had a girl working for him

Barry and Kathleen at their desks. 1960s.

named Doreen and he sent her down for a couple of weeks to show us how to go on.

At the time of his death my father had seven vehicles and I knew that I'd got to make a success of running the business. The hours were horrendous; some nights I didn't go home. I used to do a lot of steel from John Summers in Shotton and there were nights when I'd jump in a wagon and load it just to save a wage.

At this time the base was In Vernon Road, Stoke. Domestos owned the building and father had rented a third of the garage. After his death I wanted to expand the business which I did, very quickly. The Michelin Tyre Company was our major customer but we soon built up a large customer base. We'd gone from seven vehicles to twenty and we'd outgrown the site. I'd got all these vehicles parked in

Special 'A' Licence Lorries to cover any distance

London – Liverpool – South   Coast

Telephone: 47691-2

Telephone after Business Hours: Newcastle Staffs 66166

A. & H. DAVEY (Roadways) LTD.

VERNON ROAD, STOKE-ON-TRENT

Vernon Road and needed to find somewhere else.

When the Gas Works came up for sale by the old Stoke City football ground I bought it and was planning to develop it. No sooner had I bought it than Domestos asked me to buy their site which I agreed to do and then a piece of land opposite came up for sale and I bought that too. I was now fixed up for property. It's hard to believe, but almost immediately after that the council served a Compulsory Purchase Order on all three sites to make way for the D Road. This would be about 1970. I was back to square one.

In those days drivers didn't have cars like they have today; most of them walked to work so I didn't want to be far out of Stoke. I'd seen a site in Boothen Old Road but the council said I couldn't have it. I said that I might as well close the business. My accountant produced the figures of my accounts for the previous year or two and told them how much it would cost them if I went out of business. Anyway, they finally agreed to let me buy the site.

I had to agree that within three years I'd demolish the nine Nissen huts (140' long and 40' wide) that were on the site and erect a garage. In less than the three years I demolished the huts and built a 50,000 sq ft warehouse for the Michelin. Needless to say, it took the council so many years to pay me that the interest they owed was as much as the original purchase price - at that time interest rates were running out of control. I demolished the huts and built the warehouse before drawing a penny from them.

Davey's drivers were very tough but extremely generous. For several years each member of staff contributed an amount each week out of their wages to buy powered wheelchairs for local children who needed them. Beech's staff did the same. We raised a lot of money for this very worthy cause. About twenty years ago we had an event at my home where we raised £10,000. It went on all day and most of the night - we had clay pigeon shooting, a fishing competition and I begged from customers to donate prizes for the stalls. Over the years we've supplied many of these chairs for young people. Peter Foden, the chairman of ERF, was involved as well.

If you worked hard in the sixties you could make a lot of money. At our peak we had 75 vehicles. I had to be there from early morning until late at night. I finished in haulage in 2005 but even now I don't feel I can take a holiday. I'm not so early into work nowadays - I'm usually here for 7.30am.

When my father died we were living at The Brampton and shortly afterwards my mother asked me to go to look at a house in Stanley with her. When she told me the price I was so surprised I said '*£12,000? Do you know I could buy three and a half eight wheelers for that?*' We moved there when I was 21. I was married at Silverdale Church on a Sunday afternoon in 1968. I couldn't get married on a Saturday because I was working - my wife, Maria, never lets me forget that. Our first house was in Longsdon; I'd bought it before I was married.

An 8 wheel ERF at the Motor Show at Earls Court in 1960, in Davey livery.

George Pritchard Sr drove this eight wheeler for Daveys in the 1960s. Arthur Davey wouldn't buy a vehicle unless the registration number had the number 7 in it. Barry tried to continue the tradition but as the fleet grew this became more difficult.

A Davey ERF coming off junction 15 of the M6 on the A500, March 1994. *John Heath*

Barry with some of his men outside Vernon Road garage. c1960. L-R: Peter Chandler, John Adams, Cliff Mould, Barry, Frank Davenport, ? , Eric Morley, Stan Riley.

The Commercial Motor Show at the NEC, Birmingham. c. 1995.
Barry (left) with Peter Foden CBE, with recipients of powered wheelchairs.

R693 FEU ERF 6x2 sleeper cab unit with a Cummins M11,
built in 1996. The trailer is an AHP coil carrier. On the rear of
the trailer is a Moffett fork lift truck. T768 RVT ERF 4x2
sleeper cab unit, again with a Cummins M11, built in 1999.
This had a Hiab crane mounted to the rear of the body and also a
drawbar trailer attached to the rear of the truck. *P T Adams*

Barry and Maria Davey c.2003.

BELOW:
ERF 4x2 sleeper cab tractor unit with a Cummins M11 engine
built in 1996. The tri-axle trailer loaded with 5 ex-army trailers.
A Moffett fork lift truck at the rear. *J Harding Collection*

Beech's Garage

As a haulage contractor I only used ERFs - my father used them too - and I had a good relationship with ERF. Our local distributor, Beech's Garage on Leek Road, Hanley, was where I bought all my trucks and parts etc. The owner was a man named Norman Beech. Norman had started the business with his father, Harry, in 1932 and in 1933 they became the first distributors of ERFs in England. They were originally based in Massey Square, Burslem but eventually built the garage in Leek Road, Hanley. Norman had an excellent reputation and was respected by all. I knew him well. He was quite a bit older than me but we got on well. We went to the World Cup in '66 together and we went to see Cassius Clay fight three times. He was best man at my wedding. Sadly, eleven months later he died.

Norman Beech, owner of Beech's Garage, seen here with his plane. Early 1960s.

Photos Barry Davey Collection

Norman's business was taken over by someone else and, unfortunately, it wasn't the same. One day I went down there to see them as we were having difficulty getting the parts we needed and had to keep going to the factory at Sandbach. Anyway, as I was getting back into my car, the owner's daughter came out and asked if I wanted to buy the company. That's how it came about that I bought it. That was in 1983 and I changed the name to Beech's Garage (1983) Ltd. I made a lot of changes and the company went from strength to strength. We moved from Leek Road to our present site in Shelton New Road in 1995. Maureen, my personal assistant, was working at Beech's when I took over and is still with me; she will have done 47 years this year.

ERF was eventually taken over by the German company MAN. In 2009 Beech's was Dealer of the Year for MAN UK as well as Dealer of the Year for ISUZU commercial vehicles.

I have a personal memento of ERF, Sandbach which I see every day - I was fortunate enough to acquire the main gates to the factory and have installed them at our present site. They mean a lot to me.

CHECKLEY COMMERCIALS: Dave Unwin

I first started driving a wagon, an old BMC tipper, when I was working for my father, Joe Unwin and his brother, Sid, at Greenfields Farm, Kerry Hill. Joe and Sid had a dairy herd but they also did cattle dealing, farm contracting and haulage. I'd left school at 15 - I was actually expelled at 13 for going to school on a motorbike but my mother got them to take me back, much to my dismay. It was the first of a number of motorbike 'incidents' when I was young. I got caught going down Jack Haye Lane on a Francis Barnett bike with two mates on the back. One of them was carrying my dog, Kim. I was up in Leek Court for 'Three and a dog on a motorbike'. I was fifteen at the time.

Joe Unwin of Greenfields Farm
with his Bedford 3 tonner, c 1948.

When I left school I had several jobs in quick succession and one of them was working as an aerial rigger. The firm I worked for also did window cleaning when the aerial job was slack and one day they had me cleaning the windows at the Morgue. I was doing OK until I looked through an open window and saw this body - I got down that ladder sharpish, I can tell you. I finished that night. Several other jobs followed but I suppose it was inevitable I'd end up working on the farm.

Joe and Sid were the first in the area to get a baler, a Jones's, and wherever they went with this baler there were always farmers and farm lads watching it work. They employed local lads; I can remember John Philbin, Barry Burgen and Graham Prime. The old BMC was used to carry hay bales. It was only short so they'd leave the backboard down and have these great, high loads 'secured' with ropes. They also used to fetch sugar beet from Shropshire on it. Every day during the beet campaign (late September until mid-February) one of them would drive over to the factory at Wellington, load up and either tip at the farm or deliver loads to local farmers for cattle feed. It would have been profitable but a lot of the time they didn't get paid.

One day Sid told me I could start doing the sugar beet trip. It was a 4 am start so I left home in my mother's Triumph Herald and got up to where they parked the wagon. They parked it at my aunt Rachel's at the top of Bagnall Bank because it would never start and you had to roll it down the bank to jump-start it. They never did put a new battery on.

Anyway, I got it going and drove through Stoke, Market Drayton and Hodnet to Wellington. I remember they always gave a lift to the factory's weighbridge man on the way in so I picked him up as normal. When I got to the factory I was able to drive straight through and get first in the queue because I had this man with me. Anyway, on to the weighbridge and round to the loading bay. In those days you had to fork the load on yourself. It would take thirty or forty minutes and you had to keep trampling it down so you'd get a decent load. After I'd loaded I went back to the weighbridge. When Sid and Joe went they'd always carry a five gallon drum of water in the cab. After they'd loaded they'd throw this water over the backboard and drive on to the weighbridge with water running out of the back. A wet load cost less. When I got back to the farm at about 9.00 am I tipped - I had to fork it off because all the trampling down had made it stick. That was my first load. At about 11.30 I set off for the second.

I did this on a regular basis, sometimes tipping at Greenfields and sometimes delivering to different farms. Farmers would never help you; they'd stand and watch you chucking it off on your own. Anyway, the season went OK but the next year I wrote the wagon off. It was a case of 'the morning after the night before' when I'd been out with my mates until the early hours. I'd got over to the factory and loaded and had just come under a bridge when a wagon came the other way. I swerved to avoid him, went up the grass verge and plunged down the embankment. The wagon was on its side with this sugar beet all over the place. I managed to get out and hitched a lift back to the factory to phone Joe. When he got over to me with the Land Rover and chain we unloaded what was left on the truck and got a local recovery guy to pull it out. Joe towed me home - it took about 6 hours. That was the end of the BMC.

Well, we had to get another truck quickly and we found one at Longton Transport Equipment for £37 10s. It was much better than the old one - it had recently had a new engine, had a five speed gearbox, two speed axle, was capable of 55-60 mph and had a decent battery so no more careering down Bagnall Bank in the early hours.

After a while I got fed up with working on the farm - I was only earning about three or four pounds a week and they'd 'forget' to pay me so I left. Later on, Joe and Sid had a big fall-out and they both went out and got driving jobs - Joe went to work for Bob Nixon at R C Nixon's in Milton and Sid went to drive for Haydons, the cattle people at Biddulph.

I got a job working for Les McCann at Thorleys. He set me on driving a little Morris FG with a threepenny bit cab - I really hated that truck. I wanted to drive one of the bigger ones but he would never let me. I was delivering wood wool all around Stoke to pottery companies like T C Wild, Doultons and Spode where it was used for packing. Thorleys would send a driver in an ERF artic down to Welshpool to bring it up and leave the loaded 33ft trailer at the depot. They went down every two days because that's how long it took me to unload it. I had to do this wood wool in the mornings and in the afternoons I delivered bags of corn or fertilizer to local farms. Again, you had to unload it yourself by hand.

A 1971 Thorley ERF with Gardner 180. *Carl Johnson collection*

It wasn't long before I'd had enough of that and decided to get a licence to drive an artic. I got a job with a local firm and the first week I was shunting steel off Shelton Bar. Then during the summer I did holiday relief on Foden eight wheelers. I'd never driven Fodens but a real problem with them was they'd got no lock on the steering. The first day I got the wagon stuck in some street in Derby going to Newstead Colliery to pick up a load of slack. Then did it again just off the weighbridge at Newstead and had to be towed out. I eventually loaded the slack and got back to the yard and was told *'you've got to do two a day or one and a half a day (a load and a set-up) and then two the next day.'*

Sometimes I'd go into Liverpool Docks to pick up bauxite, a very heavy black sand with metal in it. You only covered the bottom of the truck and you'd got your load. I used to deliver it to Edwards' behind Trent Garage, Bucknall. Some of the wagon bodies were built up with wire extensions so they could carry coke to get a full load on. One of the jobs was to run empty over to Ollerton NCC Coking plant. You had to go at midnight and get there for one o clock in the morning and you'd position your wagon under one of the hoppers while it loaded (as it was being made it would be put on your truck) and then you'd set off at about 4.00 a.m. to deliver.

At some stage I bought my own Ford Trader for £47 10s from Nixons at Silverdale. I remember working at the Sewage Works at Blurton for 17/6d an hour with this Ford. I was doing OK until the bloke driving the Drott fell out with the foreman and walked off the site. We tipper drivers were told there'd be no more work until they'd found a driver for the Drott. I said straight away that I'd drive it the next day and find a driver for my lorry. The foreman asked me if I'd done it before and I said 'Oh, yeah, no problem'. Anyway, I waited until everyone had gone home that night and jumped on the machine and drove it for about four hours. When I went back the next morning at 7.00 I was fairly competent. I must have done it well enough because I was there until the job finished, three or four months later. Obviously, my wagon had smaller loads than the others!

Well, I sold the wagon because I couldn't get regular work and went to work for C E Edwards delivering sand and gravel from Croxden to concrete batching plants around Runcorn, St Helens and Liverpool.

In about 1974, after a couple more attempts as an owner-driver and a couple of partnerships that didn't work out, I decided to start buying and selling commercial vehicles to run alongside the car sales business I'd been running since about 1970. A funny story I remember from the car days was when an old farmer came on to the pitch and bought a car. One of the salesmen took his Land Rover and a goat in part exchange.

Anyway, we started selling commercial vehicles. I'd go to the truck auctions at Measham, Rothwell and Central Motor Auctions and buy vehicles. It was hard at first and I remember the miners' strike of that year nearly wiped us out.

We had an ex-driver selling these trucks who used to keep a suit, shirt and tie and shoes etc in the office and instead of going home most nights he'd go off drinking and playing cards. He'd get changed in the office and off he'd go. Then he'd call in again on the way home, get changed into his working gear, dirty his face and hands and go home. This went on for a while until we met his wife one day who set about me demanding the hundreds of pounds 'overtime' we owed him! He left soon after that.

In about 1975/76 John Belfield rang us up when he was thinking of finishing in transport and we bought his fleet. His vehicles had always got plenty of paint on and most had got Gardner 180s or 150s - everyone wanted Gardner ERFs so we started selling them. This put us on the map. We were operating on some land we'd bought from Ewart Edwards (my old boss) on Leek Road in Hanley. We sold cars on the front and trucks at the back. Then we bought the British Car Auctions site at Checkley and very quickly ran out of money!

I remember we had a bit of good fortune when somebody wanted to buy the Leek Road site. They'd had the contract for a while and had been messing about. I was in Scotland one day and rang in to the office (no mobiles in those days) and was told our solicitor was trying to get hold of me. I was in Reliable Vehicles' office at the time trying to buy 10 tractor units that had belonged to WH Malcoms although I hadn't a clue how I was going to pay for them. I rang the solicitor and he said they were willing to sign. I told him to go ahead as I was about to spend the money.

So for the next few years I was buying and selling - either buying at auction, buying fleets of trucks from owners who were retiring or buying off receivers and selling from the depot at Checkley. I did do haulage again when I bought a couple of transport companies - John Heathcote was selling up so I bought his, and Johnny Jenks decided to sell. We ran them for a while but our main business in the early years was buying and selling. I remember we bought a lot of fleets out of Scotland including Lawsons' of Dundee - about 20 DAF tractor units and thirty 40ft trailers. Then ex-Charterhire directly off DAF - we sold a lot of these to Adams Butter. We were also buying a lot off Scotia DAF in Grangemouth. A big deal for us was when we bought 16 almost new Volvo and Merc tractor units that had belonged to Youngs Seafoods. People were queueing up to buy them because they knew what good condition they were in.

I remember a time when we were buying Roman tractor units that were ex-Abbey Hill Transport. They were MAN but built in Romania; they weren't very good. I can remember buying 170 new ones. MAN in Swindon had wanted £15,000-£18,000 each for them but I remember I gave about £5,000-£6,000 each. Harry Gill, who was with us by this time, sold them all.

I met a lot of interesting people in the wagon job - two that immediately spring to mind are Monty Webster from Sandiacre and Gordon Crompton or 'Crommie' as we called him, from Bolton. Gordon's dead now but I still see Monty and have a deal with him. He's a character. I've known him for over thirty years and we've never had a cross word. His sons deal with my son now so we're on second-generation dealing. Bobby Walton from Glasgow is another long-standing friend and business colleague.

Crommie was quite a man; the deals I did with him were unbelievable. We used to concoct these deals and our solicitors would have to do the paperwork and could hardly keep up. I had one piece of land back five times!

I remember going into his office one day and he was on the phone. He looked up, and said *'Hang on I think I've got just the man for this deal'.* He put his hand over the receiver and said *'Will you go halves with me on a 6000 ton ship?'* I said I would. Well, we bought it and what a carry-on it proved to be.

We bought it off a Receiver and I remember it was in Hull Docks. We knew nothing about ships and never realised that it would cost a fortune to keep moored in harbours. Anyway, we paid and hired a captain and crew and had it taken to Sandwich Bay in Kent. We'd only

Gordon 'Crommie' Crompton
David Crompton

seen photos of it at this time but we thought it'd be ok because it weighed 6000 tons and we'd worked out the scrap value if all else failed. We advertised it all over the world and nobody came. After three or four months we decided to go down to Kent to have a look. We wandered around for ages before we spotted this rusty old hulk. To say we were disillusioned would be an understatement.

A couple of weeks later Crommie rings me and says *'Unwin, I think I know what the problem is - you should buy ships in pairs! I've been offered another one. I think our luck's about to change.'* Unbelievably, we bought this other ship. Our luck changed all right... for the worse. This one was in Liverpool Docks. We paid for it only to discover three months later that the man we bought off hadn't paid for it and we couldn't get the registration documents. Well, we sorted that out and Crommie tried to swap the pair for a hotel in Liverpool but the deal fell through.

I remember I was coming down from Glasgow one night and called in his yard at Bolton and he tells me he's just bought 120 acres of land at Winterhill, Bolton, next to the Granada TV Mast. I didn't know at the time but it was that high up there was snow on it all year round. Anyway, I decided that no matter what he came up with I was going to do a deal with him and he was having the ships. Several hours later I owned the land and Crommie had my 50% of the ships along with a loading shovel and a Ford Capri. I also had two shire horses and a Rolls Royce.

For the next six or seven years we kept on dealing with this land; buying it, selling it or part exchanging it. Crommie had it, Bill Swires had it, Albert Waring had it and I had it. In fact, it seemed like half of Lancashire had it! It finally came to a stop when the farmer who owned the adjoining land eventually bought it after negotiating at various times with us all.

In another deal I did with him we took two Rolls Royce cars, a Mercedes car, a farm tractor and an industrial building dismantled on a trailer in Anglesey. I think he took some Volvo F10s and some tipping trailers. However, what he neglected to tell me was the sectional building had been on a trailer in a field for five years. I asked a mate of mine, John Fowler, and a helper to go down in a tractor unit one Monday morning to fetch this building and was expecting them back that night. Well, getting the trailer out proved a lot trickier than anybody could have imagined. They returned six days later! That was Crommie. All good fun.

Ros and Dave Unwin 1980s.

Dave Unwin at Leek Road site with a line-up of vehicles for sale. c.1976.

BCA auctioneer, Ken Sherratt at a sale at Checkley in 1981, Major Bircher top right. Dave Unwin at the front with his hand on the windscreen.

BELOW:
A 1971 'A' series twin steer ERF taken at Scott Lidgett Road. This was an ex-John Jenks vehicle. Registration JEH 555K. c.1977.

A line-up of used vehicles for sale at Checkley Commercials in the 1980s.

ABOVE:
Line-up of D&D Transport
of Dundee vehicles pur-
chased early 1980s off a
receiver. There were about
20 tractor units, mainly
Volvo F10s and F12s and a
few Ford box vans plus
about 40 trailers.

L-R: Dave Unwin Jr, Joe
Unwin, and Dave Sr.

D Unwin Collection

A Youngs Seafoods
Mercedes unit - one
of about 16 Merc and
Volvo tractor units
Checkley
Commercials bought
in about 1989.

BERESFORD TRANSPORT LIMITED

Ken Beresford

My grandfather, John Beresford, started his haulage business in 1900 in Tunstall, transporting earthenware in crates and casks. Some time prior to the Second World War the company developed into Beresford, Caddy and Pemberton. My father, Ken Sn, came into the business as a driver and eventually became Transport Manager. I have a distant memory of travelling with my father to the Watford factory of Scammell where he collected a new Scammell eight wheeler.

A line-up of Sentinel vehicles in Beresford's yard. *K Beresford Collection*

At the time of Nationalization BCP was absorbed into British Road Services and my father became Manager of the Tunstall depot of BRS. However, on de-nationalization he was persuaded by his wife, Hilda, to form his own company which became Beresford Transport Limited in 1953. He obtained 20-30 vehicles, mainly Bedford, Leyland and Sentinel trucks, and approached a number of manufacturers in the Potteries with a view to carrying their goods. In about 1954 he was fortunate enough to secure the transport of tiles for H & R Johnson Limited.

Derek Johnson, the Managing Director, believed in free enterprise and was sympathetic to a company like Beresfords who could give the first-rate service his company required. Johnsons

Carl Johnson Collection

A Scammell rigid 6 with Gardner engine belonging to Ken Jr's grandfather, John Beresford in the 1930s. Note the balloon tyres on the rear axle.

went on to become the largest tile manufacturer in Europe and I can remember receiving a letter every year from Derek thanking us for our excellent service.

When I finished my National Service in the RAF, I never envisaged that I would play a part in the haulage business. In fact, my life took a very different path. I went to Burslem School of Art and won a scholarship to the Royal College of Art in London where I became acquainted with many designers and well-known artists. After graduating I became a teacher at Wallasey Technical Grammar School.

In about 1957 my father asked me to leave teaching and join him in the business. He wanted me to promote the business in Liverpool, particularly as the previous company, Beresford, Caddy and Pemberton, had links with the area. I jumped at the chance of running the depot there but was thrown in at the deep end. What an experience it proved to be! I worked there for ten years independently of the Head Office in Tunstall. Liverpool Docks changed considerably with containerization in the late 1960s and at about this time I came to Tunstall to run the business.

Mr Ken Beresford senior and his wife Hilda at a Rotary Club function at the North Stafford Hotel 1960s. *K Beresford Collection*

In the 1960s Liverpool dockers had to be persuaded to unload your vehicles which made our job very difficult. Sometimes vehicles had to wait to unload for up to three days. It was almost impossible to give a guaranteed collection time for our customers. Eventually, in about 1970, we became a non-union company and formed our own in-house organisation called the United Transport Workers Organisation which enabled us to negotiate with our men without the influence of the larger unions. We couldn't have done it without the agreement of our drivers. We had the power to make our own decisions and we worked closely with the men. We had a very good working relationship with our drivers.

In 1970/71 I formed, with a Mr DPI Sergeant, BERSER Shipping - BER and SER representing Beresford and Sergeant respectively. It was a natural development to have our own shipping and forwarding company which could work with agents in every European country. The company was based in Tunstall and later in Loomer Road, Chesterton with the Head Office in Rotterdam. Eventually I sold my shares in BERSER.

Beresford Transport had 100 vehicles and 200 trailers.Our vehicles were mostly ERF, Foden, Scania, DAF and MAN. The 1970s and 1980s saw the development of the continental operation with thirty vehicles a week being sent to all parts of Europe. Our European customers included Michelin Tyre Company, Yamasaki, JCB and Dunlop.

My father died in 1973 at 62 - a popular and hard working man. In 1984 I purchased the BRS site which was next door to our own yard in Tunstall. This brought with it another 40,000 sq ft of warehousing to add to the 20,000 we already had. Later, I acquired the Gem Pottery site which was in the centre of our land. My father had sold this when our business was much smaller and I spent several years trying to buy it back before we finally struck a deal. I also bought Summerbank Service Station and land at Chemical Lane, Longport where we could park up to 90 trailers.

At its peak Beresford employed 90+ drivers and 20 admin staff as well as loaders and fitters etc. Arthur Beresford was UK Transport Manger. He was a very strong character and expected perfection from the drivers but he was very fair. Geoff Ellis was our Continental Manager and David Benbow followed Fred Bevington as Accountant. Bert Middleton was Fleet Engineer. Jokingly, if a driver rang in with a problem with their vehicle, Bert would say *'I'm glad you're there and I'm here'* or sometimes *'Let it develop'*. When Bert retired Bob Culley took over.

Ken Beresford Jr who continued to run Beresford Transport Limited and subsidiary companies after the death of his father in 1972. *K Beresford Collection*

We had quite a few characters working for us: Dave Scarlett, Len Dunbar and Stan Jukes spring to mind. We had a driver in Liverpool who decided to leave the company because he had too many drops to do. I asked him who he was going to work for and he said *'I'm working for an undertaker because it's one pick up and one drop'*. I can also remember an occasion when there had been an accident in the Mersey Tunnel. Our driver, Johnny Silcock, had to make an accident report out and under the heading Be honest, who do you blame for the accident? he wrote *'The tunnel cleaner's soap and water'*.

In the early 1990s Beresford Transport was sold and we decided to concentrate on property development. My son, Dr Anthony Beresford, is Reader in Logistics at Cardiff Business School so has continued in the family tradition of transport but in a different way. He is a consultant to the Welsh Assembly, the House of Commons and many foreign governments.

My daughter worked for Granada Television in the Film Research Department for a time and now creates period costumes for museums throughout the country.

A Sentinel purchased from British Road Services (Shropshire registered) loaded with flint stones from the south coast, used by H & R Johnson Tiles Limited. *Carl Johnson Collection*

Shown across 2 pages

This picture shows lorries in Beresford's yard purchased from British Road Services at Stockport in 1953.
K Beresford Collection

A 1960s 4 wheel Bedford S type being loaded with tiles and crates of earthenware destined for Liverpool Docks.
John Heath Collection

A Beresford Caddy and Pemberton ERF John Heath Collection

BELOW:
This ERF was registered on 1st May 1957, converted in-house to a tractor unit in the mid sixties.
K Beresford Collection

A 1950 ERF - this was one of the first attempts of showing the customer's name on a headboard. John Heath remembers driving this.
John Heath Collection

Stan Jukes in Italy in about 1980/82.
Stan Jukes

Beresfords acquired Rutland Bulk Transport Ltd as well as Percy Hall & Co Ltd and Webb Bros. (Tunstall) Ltd.
Roger Kenny Archive © Roundoak Publishing.

UNIT	DRIVER	TRAILER	DESTINATION	XX DEPOT	SAILING TIME
WKE 225 X	L SMITH	H 741	INNSBRUCK+GRAZ AUSTRIA	SUNDAY 0500	SUNDAY 1330 DOVER ZEEBRUGGE
BVT 410 Y	J BAMBURY	SF714	KOLN+MOERFELDEN GERMANY		
WKE 224 X	G RODZEWICZ	K 649	CLERMONT FERRAND FRANCE		
GRF 250 V	M SIMPSON	K 614	CLERMONT FERRAND FRANCE	SUNDAY 0700	SUNDAY 1500 PORTSMOUTH HAVRE
XRE 731 S	K GREEN	H 704	CLERMONT FERRAND FRANCE		
LRE 620 V	M DARLINGTON	H 724	CLERMONT FERRAND FRANCE		
BRF 128 T	D PARKER	H 734	NANCY+DIJON FRANCE		
NRF 407 W	M MULROONEY	H 729	BESANCON FRANCE	SUNDAY 1200	SUNDAY 2200 SOTON HAVRE
NRF 406 W	A SHAW	H717	HAVRE FRANCE		
UVT 937 X	H WINKLE	H 716	HAVRE + ROUEN FRANCE		
DVT 891 T	P WILDING	K 646	HAVRE FRANCE	SUNDAY 1400	SUNDAY 2300 SOTON HAVRE
NRF 409 W	M SALT	H 710	HAVRE + PAVIA ITALY		
DVT 979 T	A DALE	H 743	PAVIA ITALY	SUNDAY 0900	SUNDAY 1800 DOVER BOULOGNE
NRF 405 W	I ROBINSON	N 801	BURGDORF SWITZERLAND		
LRE 621 V	J DURBER	H 707	BASLE SWITZERLAND		
DFV 911 W	A AVEYARD	SF715	HAMBURG GERMANY		
BRF 129 T	J HASSALL	H 708	HOBOKEN+ZAVENTEM BELGIUM	SUNDAY 1000	SUNDAY 1900 DOVER ZEEBRUGGE
GRF 255 V	A BOOTH	H 735	HANNOVER GERMANY		
EVH 345 W	D SCARLETT	N 804	HASSELT+VILLERS BELGIUM		
BRF 127 T	M CADDICK	H 737	BELGIUM(+ DUTCH		
XRE 733 S	J STUBBS	K 615	HAVRE FRANCE	MON 0700	MON 1500 PORTSMOUTH HAVRE
BRF 125 T	S PORKIN	H 711	WOLFSBURG GERMANY	MON 1000	MONDAY 1900 DOVER ZEEBRUGGE
XRE 732 S	R JOHNSON	H 700	BAD KREUZNACH GERMANY		
AFA 612 X	J WARBURTON	SF720	MILAN ITALY	MON 0900	MONDAY 1800 DOVER BOULOGNE
			WEEKEND 6 & 7TH NOVEMBER 1982		

A trip list showing vehicles, drivers and destinations etc. 1982. *John Heath Collection*

A group of drivers at the Beresford Dinner Dance with their wives and girlfriends.
Back L-R: Harry Johnson, Alan Copestick, John Heath, ?, ?, Richard Ibbs. *John Heath Collection*

BERESFORD TRANSPORT LTD.,
RUTLAND BULK TRANSPORT LTD.,
PERCY HALL & CO., LTD.,
WEBB BROS. (TUNSTALL) LTD.,

HIGH STREET,
TUNSTALL,
STOKE-ON-TRENT.

TELEPHONE - STOKE-ON-TRENT.   88641/2/3/4 & 84,809. & 88224.

R E M E M B E R   E F F I C I E N C Y.

EASY TO FORGET THE FOLLOWING:-

FUEL, OIL AND WATER LEVELS.

FLASHERS, LIGHTS AND COUPLINGS.

INSPECT YOUR VEHICLE THOROUGHLY.

CHECK BRAKES AND STEERING.

IS YOUR ALARM WORKING.

ENSURE THAT YOUR LOAD IS SHEETED
                 AND SAFELY ROPED.

NUMBER PLATE INTACT.

COLLECT YOUR DELIVERY NOTES FROM
                     OFFICE.

YOU REPRESENT - BERESFORD TRANSPORT LTD.,

DON'T FORGET!

The front of a booklet produced by Beresfords for their drivers.
John Heath Collection

BELOW:
Beresford ERF in the days when they were painted red.
Peter Davies

Top left: John Heath with PVT 646R broken down in St Pölton 1977. You can just see the breakdown vehicle sent over from Stoke. *John Heath*

Top right:Three of the Beresford office girls: L-R: Joan, Julie and Jean. *John Heath Collection*

Right: Beresford men. L-R: Ray Morris, Tony McDonagh, Dave Scarlett, Fred Stark, Colin Manifold. K *Beresford Collection*

BELOW: A Beresford ERF (PVT 646R) driven by John Heath loaded with balers in France. c.1976 *John Heath*

Beresford Fodens and ERFs with an H & R Johnson AEC, at Johnson's premises in the 1960s. From front: K Fellows driver for H & R Johnsons, Bert Middleton, Fleet Engineer, George Moreton, John Smith, Ambie Smith, ?. *K Beresford Collection*

H & R Johnson had their own drivers - Wilf Bradbury was working for Richards Tiles when they amalgamated with Johnsons in 1978. Wilf continued with local work with the occasional exhibition job when he took ware to the Ideal Home Exhibition in London. This was taken in 1981. In 1983 Johnsons sold all the lorries off with the contract going to Browns of Tunstall. Wilf continued to work for them. *Wilf Bradbury Collection*

A London trunk lorry loading tiles in the 1960s at central warehouse (H & R Johnson) John Heath Collection

The sale catalogue when Ken Beresford finished in transport to concentrate on property development.
CVA conducted the auction in April 1994 at the depot in Tunstall.
Dave Scarlett Collection

Under instructions from
BERESFORD TRANSPORT LTD
following a decision to reduce their UK Operations
and concentrate on their European Operations

COMMERCIAL
VEHICLE
AUCTIONS

COMMERCIAL VEHICLE AUCTIONS LTD.

will sell by auction, on the premises at

BERESFORD TRANSPORT LTD
HIGH STREET
TUNSTALL
STOKE ON TRENT

ON SATURDAY, 30th APRIL, 1994
AT 11.00 a.m.

88 COMMERCIAL VEHICLES & TRAILERS

**TRACTOR UNITS
RIGIDS
TILTS, PSK FLATS
CURTAINSIDERS
BOX VANS**

BELOW:
The sale line-up.
John Heath Collection

John Heath

I was 19 when I started at Beresfords as a trailer-mate and 21 when I started driving. I was on a van for a while then an Albion four wheeler and a six wheeler before I went on to artics.

In 1974 I started driving abroad. One journey I remember very well was when a group of us were in France. I'd tipped my load and was due to load these tic-tac mints at a place in between Rouen and Le Havre. However, if you weren't there for a certain time of day they wouldn't load you so everybody used to congregate at Rouen on what we used to call the Wine Cellars where the tankers came in with wine. There were quite a few of us: Stan Jukes, Johnnie Durber, Phil Coomer - I think about eight of us altogether. Anyway, we went to this restaurant at about four in the afternoon and then someone said *'Let's go up the town'*. So we dropped two trailers and left them there and off we went in these two tractor units.

Well, we'd had a few drinks and it must have been getting on towards midnight when we decided to get back. Where were the lorries? We couldn't find them. Anyway, we started walking and singing and fooling about and the gendarmes come round the corner in this van. They got me, Johnny Durber and two others. They said we were causing a disturbance and bundled the four of us in this twelve-seater van. I think they handcuffed us together. Then this big Alsatian dog gets in. They took us off to the police station and put us in a cell with this Frenchman. They took everything off us - shoes, belts and wallets.

There was absolutely nothing to sit on. Up in one corner was this toilet; one of the old fashioned French toilets with just two foot marks and a hole. Every minute or so it flushed. What a night. They did give us food but it was awful - the only thing I had was an apple. The next morning they took us away to another station which was more like a small jail. We really thought we were going to end up in court. It was some time in the afternoon when we were set free. We didn't really know what had happened but someone must have reported us missing or something. I think the agent had to get someone belonging to the British Embassy to get us out. When they released us they took us back to the first police station and gave us our belongings. We walked down the road and there were the lorries just where we'd left them!

John Heath being helped by Mr Joe Bamford (founder of JCB) when John delivered some items to his villa in Majorca.
John Heath

On the 24th August 1980 I went to Majorca with a load of personal items for Mr J Bamford, the founder of JCB. I'd known for a few days that I was doing this trip (lucky me) so my wife at the time, Mary, decided to come along. I was driving an Atkinson, 400, GRF 254V in JCB colours.

We caught the Brittany ferry from Plymouth for Santander, Spain; it was a 24 hour sailing so we didn't arrive until late on Monday afternoon. On the Tuesday we drove to Barcelona - a long drive on those Spanish roads in 1980 - and, as we'd missed the Tuesday night ferry, spent the day in Barcelona and caught the Wednesday night sailing to Palma. We got a bit of a shock when we got on this ferry because it was a 'freight only' vessel and the facilities left a lot to be desired.

When we arrived at Palma Ferry Port we contacted Shorts, the shipping agents, and were told we couldn't clear customs until the Monday. This was bad news; we had no choice but to leave the trailer on the dock and drive off in the tractor unit to find a hotel to stay in. When we'd sorted out our hotel we let the agent know where we were staying. Shortly afterwards we got a message from Mr Bamford telling us to go down to Port Andratx the next morning (Friday) to meet him. We were told to look for a Ford Granada, registration no. JCB 888. When we got there he introduced himself and told us he'd arranged for us to stay in another hotel and that the bill had been taken care of! He told us to call him Joe.

Over the weekend we went to his villa to see if we could get the trailer up there but the road was too narrow and steep so he said he would arrange for some smaller lorries to trans-ship the items on to. We had a great weekend; we were wined and dined and had a trip on 'Elibyrd', his boat.

We went down to Palma on the Monday and managed to get clearance. The next day we drove to Port Andratx and waited for the lorries to arrive. It took all day to transfer the boxes, furniture and the two big anchors and chains on to these lorries. When we'd done we thanked Mr Bamford for his very generous hospitality and said our goodbyes. It's a trip I'll never forget.

We got the night ferry on Wednesday back to Barcelona and went to a factory south of the city where we collected 20 tons of plastic pellets. So it was homeward bound to Blighty via France and across to Dover from Calais.

Dave Scarlett

When I first started driving I was working for Co-op Bread but I moved to their dairy at Sneyd Green for more money. I was working seven days a week driving a Ford Thames. I went to work for Beresfords in 1972; I'd already got my HGV Class 3 but I got my Class 1 while I was there.

When I started driving on the continent there were no sleeper cabs; you had to make a sort of bed with a board. I'd take a big box with food and water in and a bowl to have a wash in somewhere. My first trip was over to Holland. A group of us went: Tony McDonagh, he's dead now, Johnny Pye, Johnny Heath, Johhny Durber might have

Dave Scarlett's sons Lee (left) and Mark standing in front of a Beresford Foden, c.1980. *Dave Scarlett*

Dave Scarlett delivering JCBs to Ullstrattan, Holland in the late 1970s.
Dave Scarlett Collection

been with us and Ivan Derricot who's dead now and a bloke named Norman, I think he came from Market Drayton.

Anyway, I did a few trips overseas and one day they sent me down to Germany with a load of Michelin tyres. I tipped and got to a place near Ludwigshafen ready to load timber back for Fraylings at Longport. It was winter and I'd got to stay the night in the cab. I'd got my big PMT coat on and was in a sleeping bag. I put the gas stove on and I'm lying there and I've never been as cold in my life as I was that night. At 5.30 the next morning the gas fire had gone out and the inside of the wagon was thick ice. The trailer sheet was frozen stiff - it was a tilt trailer. I tried to fire the lorry up but it was frozen. No heating at all. Anyway, I eventually got loaded at about dinner time. I decided there and then that no matter what happened I was going home. I got to Dover and there was a telex message: Dave Scarlett, don't leave Dover, stay there! They obviously wanted me to do another trip but I wasn't going anywhere else in that wagon. I rang home and said to my wife, Chris, *'It looks like I'm going to get the sack - I'm coming home. This load's for Stoke and it's going to Stoke.'*

On the Monday morning I had to go in to see Harold Dale. He took me off continental work and I had to ask Arthur Beresford for a UK job. Anyway, I was given a Big J to drive in the UK. Then I started to do the odd continental job if they needed me to and eventually did it full time. I drove on the continent for about fourteen years altogether. I had the first MAN truck and Mr Beresford had his granddaughter's name, Sophie, written on it. This would be about 1984.

Beresfords finished in 1994. Me, Freddie Stark, and Tony Mountford were there until the end. We got all the wagons ready for the sale on 30 April. My rig, B370 MRE an MAN, fetched £3000.

Jimmy Stubbs

I started driving when I was 17 for British Railways at Stoke. Over the years I've worked for quite a few of the local hauliers including Daveys, Morgans, Beresfords and Warburtons. When I was on Beresfords I started going abroad for them for more money. When you first go over it's exciting but I took headache tablets every day for about a month because it's so stressful. Germany, for example, is confusing with the motorways and you lose your sense of direction and, of course, you're driving on the right hand side of the road. You had to get what they called a T form stamped as you went through the different countries. I remember a driver who went to Switzerland and he had his papers stamped but he didn't realise that he'd dropped his top sheet on the floor. After driving about ten hours to Calais he put his papers in and they asked for the top copy with the stamp on. Well, he hadn't got it and he had to drive all the way back to Switzerland where, luckily, he found it on the floor where he'd dropped it.

We used to play tricks on each other all the time. I remember one when you'd parked up somewhere and you needed to close your eyes for a bit. You'd leave your engine running, put your arms over the steering wheel and rest your head and have a quick fifteen minutes' kip. Someone would see you, pull in facing you, put their headlights full on, rev the engine and blare the horn. You'd wake up and see what you'd think was a wagon coming at you and you'd be standing on your brakes, Another trick was when you were lying down on your bed in the cab at night and someone would climb up on to the roof and hang over the side of the cab with a torch. They'd be banging on the roof *'I'll have you out in a minute, driver.'* You'd wake up and think you'd tipped over.

I'm retired now but I miss driving - I got to meet so many people. In recent years I've organised reunions for all the Stoke continental drivers. 200 people turned up for the first one I did.

Phil Bunch

When I first started driving on the continent I was working for Beresfords, a man named Denis Holford got me started. I actually worked for Ken Beresford Snr; young Ken was in the office in Liverpool then. His old man was a gentleman. He could be funny at times. One bloke went to him once and said *'Boss, is there any chance of me having a radio in that wagon?'* The old man looked at him, pushed his hat back and said *'Son, if you're lonely, learn to whistle.'* If you'd had a radio in those things you wouldn't have heard it anyway - you wouldn't have heard Foden's brass band if it was stuck

Phil Bunch and Stan Szavaski near the Maas tunnel in Rotterdam. 1970s. *Phil Bunch Collection*

on the back. Some of the people I remember from Beresfords are Paddy O'Neil, Jimmy Lofthouse, Alan Copestick, Denis Holford, Dickie Ibbs, Edgar Childs, Stan Szavaski (Stackatrucksie) and Daft Hat - he used to wear a hat that looked like it was moulded to his head.

Alfie Booth

I started to work for Beresfords in about 1973. I was doing local at first but in the 1980s they started doing international work and I drove abroad for them for about thirteen years. They were a good crowd of men on Beresfords - you'd get to know others from different companies as well. In international work it was far better than in England because even the competition would stop and help you out. In the 80s and 90s Chapman and Ball and Comart were more or less finishing then. Moorlock from Stoke were going - they used to haul Kodak films in refrigerated vans.

I remember going through France one day and one of Belgates from up Yorkshire was just behind me. CBs had just come out and I said *'Belgate, you've just lost a wheel'*. He said that he hadn't. I said *'You have, it's just passed me!'* I was in a cafe in France one day and I'm queuing up to pay and Arthur Sproston who drove for Carmans is behind me and says *'By, you're eating well Beresfords'* and I said *'Yes, I'm not doing so bad, Arthur, am I?'* As I got up to the kiosk to pay I said *'He's paying' and walked off.* He said *'I've got to pay for your cheek!'* They were good days.

On 6 March 1987 I was in Zeebrugge waiting to get on the ferry to get back to Dover. Vehicles were boarding the Herald of Free Enterprise and I would have been one of them had it

not been for a problem getting my T Form stamped up. I was about six short of getting on that boat. The Herald left its berth at about 6.00pm and quickly capsized - I think nearly 200 people died. When it was announced there were police and fire engines everywhere. I rang home at about 7.20 and told my wife what had happened and that it would be on the news but I was OK. When we passed it the next day the water was very still; everything was still. I'll never forget it.

Alfie Booth washing his vehicle off next to Dave Scarlett's MAN - this was the first MAN in the Beresford fleet and had Mr Beresford's granddaughter's name, Sophie, written on it. *Dave Scarlett*

The KS Diesel Lorry

Kerr Stuart & Co Limited was a locomotive engineering company based at California Works, Whieldon Road, Stoke on Trent. The engineer and writer, L.T.C. Rolt, was serving an apprenticeship at Kerrs during the development of the KS diesel lorry and gives an interesting account of it in his book *Landscape with Machines*. The KS is believed to be the first British production diesel lorry - there were other diesel lorries on the road before it but these were converted steamers. However, a few months after its launch in 1929 the company collapsed.

A NEW TYPE OF DIESEL LORRY was the heading above *The Times* report of the March 1930 AGM. During this meeting the chairman, Herbert Langham Reed, stated that the KS 7 ton diesel lorry had met with considerable success and that *'on a five-day weekly run of 600 miles per week it had showed an annual saving of over*

This photo of the KS with J Beresford & Sons written on the bonnet is taken from a trade journal of 1930. *Richard Stannier Collection*

£700 per annum as compared with a similar petrol lorry and £670 over a steam lorry.' He went on to say that the locomotive industry was so depressed it had become impossible to secure orders of any magnitude and the Board's aim was to liquidate assets, reduce the overdraft and press forward with the manufacture of the company's specialities, especially the diesel lorry.

Seventeen days later a petition for the winding up of the company was presented to the High Court on behalf of Midland Bank. The Stoke branch of the engineering union appealed to the Lord Privy Seal to use his influence to get a reprieve and he wrote to them to say the petition had been withdrawn on the 8th May. However, the company's own bankers appointed Sir Harry Peat as Receiver and Manager three days later. By this time there were 500 people employed there - a few years earlier there had been 1000 and in 1922 as many as 1200.

During the summer of 1930, whilst fulfilling orders in hand, there was still hope locally of a reconstruction of the company. *The Sentinel* reported: *'The firm exhibited their well-known KS Diesel lorry at the Royal Agricultural Show in Manchester and this aroused a gratifying degree of interest, calling forth many enquiries.'* In fact, Kerr Stuart's Sales Manager had told them that they had sold several vehicles with one in use locally, probably John Beresford's. However, the workforce was gradually reduced and the site and its plant and machinery put up for sale.

The compulsory winding-up order for Kerr Stuart was made on October 14, 1930 and at the first meeting of the creditors and shareholders in the liquidation proceedings, Mr Langham Reed attributed the failure of the company to three things: The locking up of large sums of capital in the Peninsular Locomotive Company; the presentation of the petition by Midland Bank and subsequent publicity; and to liabilities incurred by the company in supporting other companies.

Herbert Langham Reed died at his home in Berkeley Square, London three years after the collapse. He was 51. He was a director of shareholder of several companies at the time of his death including Arsenal FC.

Whatever went on at Kerr Stuart it's obvious that the 1920s were difficult years for heavy engineering and the directors' attempts at diversifying would seem reasonable in the circumstances. As well as Evos Doorways - the 'complete doorway' system - they had a substantial holding in a company producing Coalite and were looking to gain specialist business manufacturing low-temperature plant for it. The KS never really had a chance to get established so we'll never know whether it was any good or not. However, it was designed and built in Stoke on Trent so it deserves a mention in this book.

*Kerr Stuart & Co Ltd
Stoke on Trent*

A British-built Diesel-engined lorry which has lately been improved in certain respects—the K.S. seven-tonner.

Richard Stannier Collection

G & B MCCREADY: Barry McCready

My brother and I started the business in 1960 with a friend running out of the quarries. The other lad backed out shortly afterwards and left the two of us to carry on. We were both miners but I always worked in the private drift mines. Unlike the Coal Board mines that have a shaft, these slope down off the surface and you follow the seam. Originally I worked for a chap named A C H Price who had been the engineer at Holditch Colliery and had decided to set up on his own. My brother Graham was a fireman in the pit responsible for explosives. We carried on with our jobs whilst trying to run a couple of vehicles up until about 1968/70.

When we started doing haulage full-time we had about three or four vehicles doing mainly coal until we had a chance to operate a pit alongside the A34 called High Carr Colliery. There were actually six of us involved and we were doing all the haulage which was quite good at the time. We started to build the coal side up and acquired what was left of the Apedale Colliery after the Coal Board closed down.We operated as the Great Row Colliery Company Ltd. Unfortunately in about 1975 it was decided to sell out to a PLC; I was against it but I was the youngest and the odd one out so the sale went through. Part of the conditions of the sale was that we would continue to do the haulage for the company which we did for a number of years.

Apedale was a very rich valley in its day with the steel works and the coal mines. I have a huge map dated 1845 which shows all the coal seams - it's so accurate it's hard to believe they did this without the surveying equipment we have now. There was also a lot of black ash, red ash and slag which is the run-off from the steel. We used to carry a lot of slag for J Forsters the saw mill people, who owned the land it was on. This slag was white lumpy stuff that they crushed and we delivered to the contractors where it was used as a base for the roads. There was a time when all the builders were using red ash in the foundations of houses and it caused a lot of trouble. If you walk around Apedale you can see why: there are big holes that have been burnt in the ground where the ash has been. Anyway, we were hauling thousands of tons of this.

We were running eight tippers hauling mainly coal. We took it to steam railways, power stations, ICI in Manchester; Brunner Mond, Northwich; British Aerospace, Chester; and Tunnel Cement at Mold where they used it for drying the cement.

I remember we were working at High Carr one day when I came up to the top of the bank and was looking down to where we were tipping. We had a relative of ours working for us at the time and he was driving this new Atkinson we'd bought. It was the last one of this model to be made and Atkinson gave us a plaque as a memento. We also have a photograph of it coming down the assembly line with the new model right behind it. Anyway, I just turned for a second and this man tipped it on its side. My brother was having a flying lesson out of Sleap at the time and he was overhead at precisely that moment and saw the whole thing. He was back in next to no

Barry & Christine with grandchildren James and Rebecca August 2010

time! We had it fixed but retired it in 1981 when we started with Volvos.

By 1980 we had about 20 vehicles including sub-contractors and bought the site where we are now in Spencroft Road, Chesterton. It is on part of the old Durose Transport Cafe site. In 1986 we bought a bus company, Poole's Coach Company Ltd, which we ran alongside the haulage operation until the mid 1990s.

My brother Graham died in November 2008 and today the businesses are run on a day to day basis by my son Mark. The transport company operates 12 lorries providing general haulage, pallet network distribution and specialized deliveries of concrete panels throughout the UK - vastly different to when we started when we concentrated on bulk tippers delivering coal, sand and gravel. However, during the mid 1990s when all the coal mines closed we had to look to other areas of work and diversify. We also run a ceramics business and a tool supply business.

Peter Hemmings

When I first started driving I was on a bread van. I was a salesman for Champion Bakeries. We used to go all over in these old Commer lorries delivering bread; they were ex-army and had gun turrets at the top that were covered in. It doesn't seem five minutes ago. When my brother-in-law came working for Barry I came as well and I did about thirty one years.

We had a few characters who worked for us: one was a man named Albert; he drove a tipper with an automatic tailgate on the back so he didn't have to get out and fasten it up. When he used to tip his load he'd drive off while the tipper body was still coming down and then press the hydraulic button to lock it up. He was always in a rush. One day he was on Silverdale and he came out with the body still up and it jammed underneath the main gantry. The lorry went out and left the body holding the gantry up. It stopped production for about three days.It cost thousands and thousands of pounds. Anyway, Barry thought he'd make sure he was aware of what he'd caused and arranged to take him down to see the manager to apologise. The guy was shaking when he sat down. Barry said that he'd come to apologise and the manager said 'Oh, well, accidents happen!'

Atkinson Defender KVT 604P with Gardner engine. This is the very last Atkinson built - here shown as it comes to the end of the production line in April, 1975. Purchased by McCready Brothers.

A McCready Volvo FM12 moving a wide load of concrete in 2009 from Newcastle Under Lyme to the Royal Shakespeare Theatre in Stratford This formed part of the new viewing tower at the theatre.

Another shot showing a Volvo FH12 with the FM12 being escorted on the motorway.

COMART

Derek Birch

I started working for Comart, based in Longton, in 1972 and travelled to many different countries for them. When the company closed down I lost a very good job. When you're doing that sort of job you're at the top of your profession. It was a blow for me to finish but towards the end I was away so often that I rarely got to see my wife and children.

If you look at photographs of Comart's vehicles in the early 1970s they don't look dated, even today. They were painted all white and stood out from the rest. There was a Dutchman who said that you could never go a day anywhere in Europe without seeing a Comart vehicle. At the end there were about 40 vehicles - all refrigerated for carrying foodstuffs although we did sometimes bring other goods back. I can think of one occasion when we brought back a load of Gucci handbags from Italy.

I remember going for my interview with Clive Smith. He said he was having trouble with *breakdowns. He asked me, 'What's the first thing you do when you break down on a motorway?'* I said that I get my tool box out. He opened the office door and shouted to the transport manager *'We've got a bloke here with a tool box - set him on!'* That's how I got the job. That tool box was used all over Europe - sometimes they'd send me 300 miles out of my way to go and help another driver out. We were self-sufficient; I carried four weeks' supply of food besides spare parts for the vehicle and the refrigerator. If the fridge broke down for just two hours then the load would be ruined so it was important to be able to do repairs.

When I first started I was set on as a UK shunter picking up loads for export. My first trip was driving a Big J to Lockerbie and my second driving a Volvo to Northern Ireland when a driver had refused to go because of the troubles there. When I got back to the yard they told me I was going to Belgium so I went to the local Post Office and got a visitor's passport which, I think,

```
11774 YU NATION
36520  COMART G

GOOD AFTERNOON,

CAN YOU PLEASE BE SO KIND TO PASS FOLLOWING TELEX TO OUR
STARDRIVER MR. DEREK BIRCH PLEASE -/- THANKS IN ADVANCE
HELLO DEREK / ROB HERE - DETAILS AS FOLLOWS - PS SORRY FOR
DELAY BUT LINDA IS NOT IN TODAY - SO I AM A BIT BUSY - AND
COULD NOT GE T THROUGH VERY EASILY...

PLEASE LOAD  TOMORROW FROM:-

MESSRS ETOL,
COLDSTORE BAJINA BASTA
B A J I N A   B A S T A
================================

TO REPORT THERE IN ORDER OF MESSRS DE LEEUW, BRANDRECHT (HOLLAND)

FOR A LOAD OF (MIMIUMUM) 20 TONS FROZE N RASPBERRIES

CLEARENCE VIA HENK HENTZEN, VENLO E3

DELIVERY TO .......... DO NOT KNOW  - BECAUSE THERE IS A GOOD CHANGE
THAT WHEN OEE YOU HAVE BROUGHT IT INTO HOLLAND THEY WILL SEELLL THE
LOAD AGAIN TO FRANCE.... - BUT ANYWAY - LET'S FIRST SEE IF WE CAN GET
THIS LOAD ON.

PLEASE GIVE US A CALL FROM ITALY AAEE AGAIN - 0 YES - WHEN YOU
ARE AT FENETTI TO MAKE T-FORMS PLEAEEE PLEASE GO TO MESSRS

*****PARISI******* AS THEY ARE THE QUICKEST AND CHEAPEST.

BFN-ROB
36520  COMART G
11774 YU NATION
```

Telex messages were the way companies contacted their drivers when they were abroad. *D Birch Collection* lasted for a year - I later got a full passport.

In 1975 I was the victim of a hijacking in Italy. At this time a lot of trucks were being hijacked because meat was such a high price but things like loads of whisky were also vulnerable. I remember following a Scottish driver down the motorway one day and we pulled off at the same services and got chatting. He wanted to know who'd been hijacked on Comarts and, of course, I told him it was me. He was carrying whisky regularly to Italy and he told me he was ex SAS. He was set on, presumably, because he knew how not to get hijacked. He mentioned that he carried a gun; he left it in Dover when he came in to this country and picked it up again when he went out.

There was one occasion when an Irish driver had pulled up on some services (there were lots of Irish going over there at the time) and he'd fallen asleep and woke up with someone banging on the door. He'd got a fire under his back axle. So he jumped out of his wagon and hijackers hit him over the head, put him in his sleeping bag and tied him up. They put a gag in his mouth and pushed him down the ditch at the side of the car park. Then they took his wagon. It took him three days to get the gag off before he could shout anybody.

There was a driver up in Austria who got gassed. He'd got the air vent open on the roof and they gassed him. They took his lorry and left him at the side of the road where he died.

I'd got a load of beef on from Ireland and I must have been followed when I stopped at services north of Milan for a break. I came back to the wagon and as soon as I put the key in the door there was a bloke behind me with a gun to my head. Another man pushed me over the diesel tank and tied my hands behind my back. It was quick. People could see what was going on but they didn't want to know. I hadn't parked in a quiet place; it was busy. It was an automatic hand gun and he started to speak in German. He was a tall bloke and while they were tying my hands he said in bad English, *'You speak, I shoot'*. I was looking at the gun and his hands were shaking so much, I really thought he would shoot me. They had to force me up into the cab because I couldn't do anything with my hands behind my back. I was pushed over the seats into the sleeping compartment. Once I was in the back the bloke with the gun got in the driving seat and the other man got in the passenger side and they drove off.

After we'd left the services and travelled so far up the motorway we came up to a payage point where you pay for the motorway. That's when the gag went in my mouth and they pointed the gun between the gap in the curtains to make sure I didn't try to attract attention. They did this at every payage. These payages have armed police on duty and all hell would have let loose if I'd shouted.

It was about seventeen hours altogether from Milan down to Naples; it was late afternoon when the journey started so they drove through the night. I could understand some of what they were saying and he was telling his mate, every time an English lorry passed, to *'Wave, wave. The English always wave'* to make it look like there was nothing wrong.

Although they'd drawn the curtains between the sleeping compartment and the front of the cab I could still see through a small gap so I was well aware of where we were going. I also realised that there was a third man in a Volkswagen. This vehicle would get in front every so often and they would flash their headlights.

I was let out at one point where I was allowed to go to the toilet at the side of the vehicle but that was the only time in all those hours. They filled up with fuel using the money that was in my file - about £1000 in foreign currency. We always took cash to pay for things like the Mont Blanc tunnel and diesel etc. so this wasn't unusual.

Anyway, they carried on down to Naples. They went around to the docks for some reason or other and were talking to various people - I couldn't understand all that they were saying but I gathered they were looking for vehicles to transfer the load on to. They couldn't turn up with my truck to the abattoir or wherever they were planning to take it because they would be found out. Eventually they came out of the docks and parked up on a lay-by at the side of the motorway.

The man who had been passenger was now given the gun and the other two went off in the Volkswagen. After about an hour he started to get anxious; his mates had left him and he was on his own. The police were passing all the time and the English drivers were blowing their horns. There was room for another vehicle to pull up behind us. Anyway, he got more and more agitated and decided to make a move. He tied my feet to one seat and my hands to the other and left me. He'd gone, I presumed, to look for his mates.

I'd spent all these hours twisting and stretching this wire around my wrists and as soon as he left I managed to slide my hands out. I was free. They'd left all the documentation behind including my passport etc. I took the fuses out of the truck so they couldn't restart it and ran up the road to try to stop someone. It would be about midday by this time. I'd just managed to stop an army vehicle full of soldiers when I noticed the Volkswagen; they could see I'd escaped and quickly sped off.

The man in charge phoned the police who raced me off to the police station. I tried to explain to them what had happened but there was obviously a language problem. I asked for a drink of water and they got me one in a small plastic cup. I hadn't had a drink for seventeen hours so asked for more and they wanted to know why I kept asking for water!

Eventually they got someone who could translate and I explained what had happened but it was fairly obvious that they thought I was involved in some way. When I told them that the boss of the gang was about 6 ft tall they said there aren't any Italians that tall. I said I thought he came from the Balzano area because he also spoke German. They didn't believe me one little bit. They asked me why I hadn't shot them. I said that I didn't have a gun. They said, *'Every driver in Italy carries a gun, where's yours?'*

They took me back to the wagon and started to search inside the cab. The driver had left his jacket on the back of the seat and they pulled it out and said 'Here's your jacket'. It was enormous. I said 'No, that's not mine; it belongs to the bloke with the gun'. Eventually, they realised I was telling the truth when they found his I.D. in the pocket.

At this point the vehicle wasn't locked up and I didn't have any keys as they'd taken them. However, I'd had this truck from new and, as luck would have it, the steering lock wasn't working so I was able to hotwire it and drive it back to the police station. Then I had to sit in the back of a police car between two policemen with machine guns. They wound the windows down each side and the driver in front said we were going to look for the bandits and told me to 'Point if you see them'. So we were chasing around Naples and I'm wondering how on earth I was going to do this. It was a fiasco. This went on for a couple of hours.

I contacted the office and asked them to get some money to me so I could continue with the journey which they did. I was at the police station for about twenty four hours and during this time they were insisting I turn the fridge of the vehicle off because of the noise. Anyway, I kept turning it back on because I was very worried that when I did eventually get to the destination the meat would be rejected. It was a boiling hot day and the police kept insisting I turn it off. At one point I had to get them out to show them that blood had started to run all over the floor. They eventually let me leave but my worry now was whether the customer would reject the load. I'd got another ten or twelve hours driving up into the North so I turned the fridge down to -4 degrees to get the temperature down as much as possible.

I got the load to the destination and remember opening the doors and seeing all this blood on the floor; I thought they'd never accept it. However, they did . After unloading I washed the vehicle out and was so glad to get away that I forgot about the hose - I drove off and ripped it out of the ground.

When I got back to England they gave me a week off and said they wouldn't send me back to Italy for another month. My next load was for Holland so I arrived and unloaded and they reloaded me but what I didn't realise was that it was for Milan. I rang them up and said *'You've loaded me for Italy'*. They said *'Sorry, Derek, we've tried everything, we can't find a load for you anywhere else'*. So I had to do it.

I went to Milan via the Brenner; it wasn't a regular route for UK drivers so I was on my own. When you go on a regular route you see other English drivers. Once I'd got through to Italy I started to think I was being followed so I was pulling in on every service station to see if the lights were following me. They weren't. It was in the early hours of the morning when I got to Milan. It's best, when travelling in Milan, to drive at night when it's quiet. Anyway, I was on this road and wasn't sure which way to go when I noticed a building with a small window, something like a little pigeon hole, with a light on. I could see a bloke inside; he looked like he was reading. I assumed he was a night watchman so I took my documents out with the address on, crossed the road and knocked on the window. I pointed to the destination I wanted and he opened the window and pointed a gun at me. He was waving it about telling me to go away. I quickly jumped in the wagon and drove off. I did eventually find the place I needed to be and delivered the load.

The only reason the hijacking came to light in this country was that I had to give evidence in Leek Court and the newspapers picked up on it. After the police had caught the perpetrators they wanted me to go over there to give evidence and the expenses that they offered me amounted to the price of a meal a day. I could have been down there for three to four weeks with no pay and I would have to find my own way down there! Eventually, they agreed that I could give evidence in Leek Court about twelve months later. I don't know what sentences they received.

As most drivers will tell you, driving on the Continent is very tricky because of the corruption. The police would stop you in France just because you were English. They knew you'd come over on the ferry and would have bought a bottle of whisky so they'd stop you for it. You'd get two bottles so you could put your foot down and if you were stopped you would be 'fined' a bottle of whisky. But they'd stop you when you'd done nothing wrong. When Unilever took over Comart, one of the blokes in charge didn't believe that we had to do these sorts of things. He went to Italy on holiday and got summonsed for speeding. He got back and got talking to one of the drivers and said he'd paid his fine and hadn't had to bribe the policeman. The driver looked at the receipt, turned it over and said *'You've been done. He's given you a receipt that means nothing. He's pocketed the money he's had off you'*.

The Italian police used to open the back up and take stuff. I remember it was a red hot day and they'd opened up the back and I was carrying Petit Pois. So they took a sack and put it in the back of their car. They wouldn't have lasted an hour before they'd thawed out but it was the way they were, they had to have something.

Driving abroad isn't for everyone. I've been with drivers and they've left England in high spirits. I've parked up in a lay-by behind them and in the morning I've had a knock on the door. *'I'm off home'*. They'd get homesick. I'd have to ring the firm up and say *'I can't stop with your*

An impressive line-up of Comart vehicles in Portugal. c. 1976.
B Brindley

vehicle but your driver's abandoned it. I've put the fridge on; you'll have to send someone out for it'. Some drivers just couldn't cope with being away from home.

At one time we were doing a lot of trips to Lisbon. We'd leave six at a time, so we'd run down in convoy. Anyway, this particular time I was feeling unwell. I was getting dizzy spells and sweating. When we got down there we caught up with six other drivers and I was last in the convoy of twelve. I knew I wasn't going to get a quick load back as I would have to wait for the others to be loaded before I could get done. All I'd got in my mind was that I had to get back home and get checked out. The route back was through Badajoz on the border of Portugal and Spain. I remember going through the border at Spain and pulled up at the first lay-by I came to, less than half a mile down the road. Arthur Johnson, another Comart driver, pulled up behind me and we parked up for the night. I didn't realise at the time that I'd stopped right outside a hospital. I went to bed for the night in my cab. In the morning, Arthur came to my cab and tried to wake me up but I didn't respond. He went to the hospital and a doctor came back down with him. All I can remember was being lifted out of the cab by this doctor and Arthur. The next time I came round I was in a hospital bed and the doctor was asking me where I was bleeding. Apparently, I'd lost a lot of blood. I must have passed out again and when I woke there was a tube coming out of my arm - I was being given blood. Standing at the bottom of the bed was a policeman, an army officer and the doctor. I couldn't understand what was going on. The doctor said that they hadn't got any blood at the hospital which was the same group as mine so they had contacted the police and the army to see if any of their personnel were compatible. These two men had donated blood to me. They'd come to the hospital to see whose life they'd saved. I'll never forget it.

I started to recover but the doctor was determined that I wasn't going to drive home and wouldn't let me out until he was sure I was going to be flying home. Within days Comart had sent a wagon down with an airline ticket. I got a lift in a Comart wagon to Madrid airport and flew home. Once I'd got home I went to the doctors and he explained that I'd got a stomach ulcer that had been bleeding over a period of time. I'd lost so much blood that I'd fallen into this coma. If it wasn't for Arthur Johnson I would probably have died in my cab.

BRITISH COMMUNITY EARTHQUAKE RELIEF OPERATI

ALLE COMPETENTI AUTORITA ITALIANE

Si attesta che il Signor D. BIRCH
è il conducente del veicolo targato AOC 471 T
che trasporta merci destinate ai sinistrati delle zone ter
remotate dell'Italia meridionale. (Materiale e oggetti
casalinghi).

Si pregano le autorità di frontiera di voler accorda
re al predetto ogni agevolazione doganale.

Si prega chi di competenza di voler esentare il predetto conducente dal pagamento del pedaggio per l'uso delle
autostrade.

Il predetto è tenuto a consegnare le merci al seguen
te indirizzo: Consolato Britannico, Napoli. Sig. Campbell

Una copia della presente dichiarazione deve essere
firmata dal ricevente.

(Luigi Orsi)
Intendente - Ambasciata d'Italia
Londra

TO WHOM IT MAY CONCERN.

TRANSLATION

Mr. D. Birch
is the driver of the vehicle reg. number AOC 471 T
and is carrying goods for the victims of the earthquake
area of Southern Italy. (household goods)

The Italian Authorities at the frontier of entry are
asked to grant all possible assistence.

It is also requested to whom it may concern to exemp
the above mentioned person from payment of motorway toll
charges.

The goods should be delivered at the following addre
British Consulate, Naples, Mr. Campbell.

A copy of this declaration should be signed and rece
by the person whom the goods are handed over.

(Luigi Orsi)
Administration Officer - Italian Embassy
London.

On 27 April 1981 Derek took a load of household goods over to Southern Italy for the victims of the earthquake in Irpinia which had occurred the previous November. This letter gave him exemption from payment of motorway toll charges. When he arrived at his destination the whole village came out to welcome him including the Chief of Police and the Mayor. *D Birch Collection*

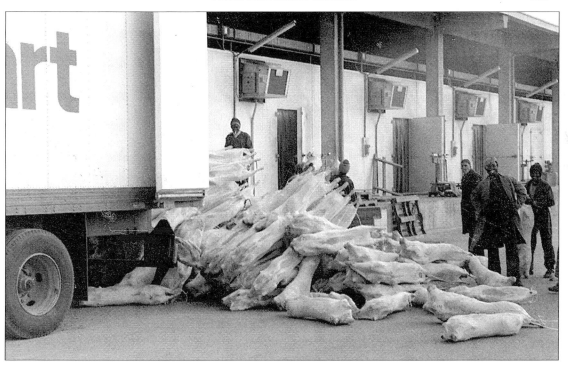

A load of meat being unloaded in Libya in the late 1970s. It wasn't unusual for a driver to be held in a compound for up to two days for passports to be checked. Sometimes hold-ups would be longer if they suspected alcohol or, as in one case, a driver having a copy of the *Sun* with a page 3 girl. *D Birch Collection*

Phil Bunch's G88 unloading at Van Den Burgs, Purfleet.
The difference between the G88 and the F88 is the front axle on the G88 is further forward. This was quite rare in the sleeper cab version. Dawson Freight of Leighton Buzzard had a good few sleepers. *Phil Bunch*

Bill Brindley

I remember an occasion in about 1976 when I was delivering a load of frozen strawberries to a place in Munich. I was driving on one of the main roads into the city centre and came to this arched bridge. I was using a street map and should have thought about it, really, because the map did show all these railway lines. It was about six-o-clock in the morning - you always tried to get into major cities before anyone was around - and I looked at this bridge and decided I could get under. Well, I did get under it but there were actually three bridges and the middle bridge wasn't arched, it went straight across. I drove up to it, got out and had a good look. I thought there was plenty of space so drove forward but what I hadn't seen was an extra RSJ holding the bridge up and I hit it.

Well, the police arrived and immediately fined me 50 marks. By this time I was causing chaos because nobody could get through. I tried to get out by letting the tyres down but it wasn't enough. With hindsight I should have just backed out but, being young and daft, I pulled forward and ripped the roof off.

When I eventually got to the other side I wasn't sure what to do but noticed a truck firm on an industrial estate. I pulled on and backed up to their metal skip. They lent me an air chisel and I cut the rest of the roof off and let it drop into this skip. All the insulation material was still there and I didn't want that to blow all over the place so I dumped that as well.

Obviously, I'd still got the strawberries on and had to get them to the delivery point so I drove with just a thin aluminium strip, like a trough, covering the load. So there was now no proper roof and no insulation and it was pouring with rain. The rain filled the trough and ran down on to the boxes but, as luck would have it, it froze and didn't cause any damage. Fortunately, when I arrived at my destination the customer accepted the load.

When I got in touch with the office they decided to send me to Holland to load with frozen peas and then swap trailers with a driver who'd brought a load of beef from England. He went back home with the peas and I took the beef to Nuremburg.

Bill Brindley in Portugal. *B Brindley*

Bill's vehicle after incident with a bridge in Munich. 1976.

CHAPMAN AND BALL

Harry Gill -

My first driving job was for a firm in Bolton called Thomas Allen. The boss, Mr Lawton, was a gentleman; he would call you 'Mr' when he spoke to you. Then I went to work for Thor running to Austria in about 1968. We were taking anything, groupage and textiles. I was tipping and loading in St Pölton in Austria, back to Manchester, tipping and loading at the same places and back again to the depot to put a few bits of groupage on and away again. That was seven days a week and probably eighteen hours a day. Nobody bothered in those days.

I was at Thor until about 1971 and then went to work for Dow Freight. The job I was doing at Thor was actually for Dow Freight and they eventually bought their own wagon. Roger Dowsy said *'H, come and drive it'*. I was working on bonus - the garment trailer held 5,000 garments but if you loaded it right you could get 7,500 in so for the extra 2,500 I got a shilling a garment.

When I left there I went to work for Dick Chapman at Chapman and Ball and started their international operation up for a 25% stake. Before I came along they were on the tipper job in the UK. Dick had taken over Chapman and Ball after splitting with Arnold Ball. Jack Correy was a director when I was there.

We were running mainly to Austria then with about five Fiats and a Volvo. I remember Tommy Robinson and Alan Meir. I think I was there until about 1975 when I sold my shares to Dick.

Ian Tyler

I remember when I started for Chapmans, Harry Gill set me on one Saturday. He told me to come in on the following Monday. I got there at 8.00am and was sent down to the Michelin in this old Guy to pick a trailer up. When I got back Harry said *'Get off home, get your gear - you're booked on the eight-o-clock boat tonight for Tehran'*. I was gone for seven weeks. This would be in 1975.

I can remember when a group of lads from Stoke were in Tehran in about 1976. There were two places where we used to go - the old customs in the middle of the city which wasn't too bad and the new customs, about 11 miles

Ian Tyler in Saudi Arabia c.1977.
The man on the left is a Belgian driver. Volvo 89.

Ian in Saudi when he was working for CAMEL - Cunard Arabian Middle Eastern Lines. 16 speed Road Ranger 6x4 ERF B Series.

outside the city, which was a hell hole. There was a piece of ground with about 300 lorries that were left there for days or weeks. There were two stand pipes for water and no toilets.

Anyway, what we used to do was drop one of the trailers and head off into Tehran. This day we went in my unit. There was Me, Ray Gould (Thor) Alan Dale (a subbie for Chapmans) and two more - I think one was John Edwards. We'd spent all day drinking in the Black Cat bar. At about 8 o clock at night we decide to go back. We all pile into this unit and set off back. The Shah had a massive monument on a roundabout with fountains and trees. Anyway, Ray Gould decides it'd be a good idea for us to climb it. After we got about 6 ft up - and you can imagine the state we were in - the police came and started to get us down. Me and Alan Dale were having shower in one of these fountains and one of these policemen points a gun at Ray. Ray says 'Eyup, that's a pistol' and took it off him, had a good look at it and gave it him back. Then more and more police arrived and they bundled us up in my wagon and sent us on our way.

After Chapmans I lived in Saudi for a while working for Cunard, the shipping line. We would pick things up from the dock off the Cunard ships and deliver all over Saudi and the Yemen. What used to happen was a ship would come in and they'd got to be turned round on the tide so everybody had to help - even if you'd been down the desert for a week.

I remember Sammy Jones from Aldridge near West Bromwich had a lot of wagons based in Saudi at the time. A lot of English lads were out there - I remember Jerry Cooke who worked for Sammy. Cunard's two top men lived in Jeddah in a posh villa and we were stuck out in the desert in two huts. But we spent most of the time in the wagon. These wagons had air-conditioning; they were ERFs with 375 Cummings. The company was called CAMEL which stood for Cunard Arabian Middle Eastern Lines. I did this for about twelve months.

I came home and worked for several other companies, including Allmans, before retiring in 2008.

A traffic jam on the road
to Damascus!

**Ian's Chapman & Ball
Volvo.**

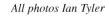

All photos Ian Tyler

BELOW:
Ian with his Ernie Owen ERF
parked up at Tower Bridge.
Alongside him is an Allmans
Seddon Atkinson driven by
Maurice Lowndes. Ian later went to
work for Allmans.

THOR: Phil Bunch

I went to work for Thor in about 1975. It was owned by two American brothers called Auden. Their main man in this country was named Markham and he was based in Wallingford which was where the Head Office was. His son, Ian, moved up to Stoke to help run the firm from this end. The office was based in Caverswall just up from the railway crossing. Originally they were in Chemical Lane in Longport. I don't know why they called the company Thor but I remember the logo was based on the Scandinavian God and underneath was written: *Thor. A thundering good service.*

We ran mainly to Iran with the occasional Baghdad. We took everything from forklifts to cooking pots. Thor was a very good firm, actually; the pay was terrible but the firm itself was good. The

Phil Bunch at Custom Car Park, Tehran
with his F88 (290) GUD 148N.

manager, Alan Dale, was brilliant - the best bloke I ever worked for. Unfortunately, he died a few years ago.

We did a bit of a spell when we were running down to the Pakistan border. We were in Iran but crossed the Great Sand Desert below Tehran to the border at Ziadam. There were quite a few trucks going down there at the time. We were taking building materials for an English firm called Marples Ridgeway. They were building a road that had been built by the British Army in 1947 but it had been virtually wiped out. When we went it was a dirt track. It used to take about 4 hours to do 100 Km, the roads were that bad. Sometimes you'd have bits dropping off your truck because you'd be bouncing all over the place with the potholes.

When you got to the Great Sand Desert they'd got three camps going across: A, B and C. When you got to the first one you'd see the Marples Ridgway Camp sign and underneath it was written *Hello, Murphy, who's sorry now?* You'd laugh at it when you were going down but when you were coming back and your truck was all in bits you'd think Dead true! Halfway across there was like a river crossing and you had to drive through it but if there was a flash flood you'd get stuck in the middle. One of the lads who did get stuck was a cockney bloke named Mick Chilley. He had to wait for the next wagon down to pull him out.

The heat on these journeys was horrendous. Obviously, we didn't have air conditioning then; it was so bad you had to wrap a rag around your hand because the plastic steering wheels got red hot. You made sure your legs didn't touch the gear stick for the same reason.

There were road signs but they were in Farsi - you learnt to understand them, though. I learnt to understand and write their numbers as well. We all had to do this otherwise you got ripped off when you stopped for fuel or whatever. We had traveller's cheques given to us from the office.

When you arrived at Iran, you put your papers in and parked up on a sea of sand - a dust bowl, really. There were trucks from all over the world parked in circles - it was like something off *Wagon Train*. You'd have the Dutch in one circle, Germans in another, English in another, French, Belgians all parked up in little groups.

Ian Adams used to be a butcher and he did all the cooking for us when we were abroad. We used to chuck a few bob in apiece and park up in Davis Turner's compound in Tehran in reasonable safety. Then he'd go up town and buy a bag of potatoes, bag of carrots, bag of onions and half a sheep. He'd butcher it and do all the cooking. We'd all got trailer boxes that the sides come down on and you'd have a stove and cooking gear in that. He'd set up a table and get the cookers all lined up. Sometimes there were springs where you could get water but mostly we used bottled water.

Everyone was waiting to tip. What you had to do was go across to the customs post at night and there was a big blackboard and if your number was on the blackboard then you'd be tipping the next day. If it wasn't on you just went back and sat it out in the wagon or we organised games of football between us and the Germans or us and the French. There was very little to do apart from going into town and going on the drink. In those days you could get drink before the Ayatollah took over.

When the Shah was in charge it was a different country. It was just like going to America. When you came into Tehran itself there were all these lean-to shacks down the side of the road selling all sorts of different stuff like blocks of ice, cases of beer or Russian vodka. Then you hit what they called the Shihad which was the Shah's monument. It was like a big roundabout with water and fountains and this great big pinnacle sticking up in the air. When you got to there you started going into like a little America, all the streets going one way had American names like Roosevelt Avenue, Eisenhower Avenue and then going crossways they were all Farsi names like Taktishamsheed which was one of the main ones.

When you wanted to phone England to let them know you were there you had to go down to the Post Office and book yourself a phone call. You had to take your number plates off while you went inside because if you were parked illegally the police used to come and take your plates off. A lot of the lads had their numbers painted on underneath so they were still there if they took them - I had mine on in Arabic.

Some of the people I remember from Thor are Ray Gould, John Edwards, Vince Biddle, Paul Elkin, Carl Cornes, Mick Chilley (Cockney Pride) John Hillihead and Mick Jackson.

Vince Biddle and Paul Elkin 1970s.

Custom Park, Tehran.
Phil's wearing the hat with Paul Elkin
back right.

Barry Morgan's White Road Boss c.
1978 - the only one in this country with
a sleeper cab.

Two Thor men on this
picture. At the back on the
right is Ray Gould; on the
right at the front is Jack
Morley. The rest we think
are Cantrells drivers.

Phil worked for Moorlock until they finished in the 1980s. He was hauling Kodak films and ships' stores to Spain, Italy, Greece, Germany and Finland. This picture shows Ray Gould's write-off in Spain.

All photos Phil Bunch

Cliff Rowley and Duncan Gould - Moorlock.

Phil Bunch (right) with Graham Jones (Honey Monster) at Customs, Dhoa 1970s.

Turkey 1970s Dave Pritchard (left) and Phil Bunch with Mount Ararat in the background.

REVS: The Register of ERF Vehicles Society

Dedicated to the promotion and preservation of the legacy of ERFoden and the products we all know as ERF. www.erfhistoricvehicles.co.uk

REVS Support Officers and Helpers at Kelsall Steam and Vintage Rally, 2011.
Back L-R: Graham Flack (Chairman), Chris Smith, (Show Co-ordinator), John Heath.
Front: Philip Hilditch, Linda Hilditch, Nicola Smith, Kevin Edwards.

This was the first ERF built, reg MJ 2711, CI4. Chassis 63.
The picture was taken by John Heath 13 July 2011 at the Cart Marking ceremony. Guildhall Yard in the City of London.
L-R: Roderick Edmund Forbes Morris (The Master Glover); Alderman Michael Bear (Lord Mayor of London); Peter
Foden CBE; Robert H Russett, (Master Carman) and Richard Foden. *John Heath*

THE NEXT THREE PHOTOGRAPHS SHOW ERF 999 NVT THROUGH THE YEARS

1. ERF KV, reg 999 NVT in Beresford livery driving in to The Motor Show at Earls Court, London, 1960. Note the
white steering wheel - this was normal for ERFs going to the Motor Show. *John Heath Collection*

2. 999 NVT seen here fitted with a box van body. *John Heath Collection*

3. 999 NVT Present day - Derek Ellis purchased this from Phil Comber and had it restored into C S Ellis colours.
Sadly, Derek died days before the lorry was completed in January this year. *Neil Cross.*

An ERF belonging to a big character in Stoke Haulage, John Jenks. John passed away last year. This photo shows his eight-wheeler coming to grief on the A39 at Knight's Mill, St Teath, Cornwall. *David M Stacey*

Chris Smith bought this 1966 LV ERF in 2003 and restored it to its former glory. It was first owned by William Boultons where it was driven by Dennis James. When Boultons went out of business Dennis bought the vehicle and converted it into a 'showroom' to take ware to trade shows. It was sold in 1987 and used by a circus touring Europe before eventually returning to Staffordshire. *John Heath*

Carl Johnson; REVS memories

Only five years old, and knee high to a grasshopper, a trip in Dad's Albion lorry of Dennis Scragg (Midlands-Scottish Transport) Cheadle fired up an enthusiasm for all lorries with ERF becoming my favourite. Why ERF? Well, I can recall my late dad telling me that ERF was the initials of a man's name, Edwin Richard Foden - the times I have heard that mis-quoted! Anyway, growing up with talk of lorries, engines, loads etc, it was no surprise to see me at the tender age of 15 leaving school and seeking employment with my beloved lorries.

The above mentioned Dennis Scragg ceased trading and the premises were occupied for a while by Vallance from Newton Abbott. I used to go down to the garage and watch the lorries leave on night trunk and delighted at the sound of those Cummins engines! My mates at this time were probably running around kicking a bag of wind about so my 'hobby' was deemed odd and resulted in it being kept low key. Summer holidays were often spent 'bagging' rides with some of the local tipper drivers. Even in those days I attended vehicle rallies and went to the local Historic Commercial Vehicle Club (and still do 41 years later).

My first job was working for Shirley's Transport of Cellarhead as an apprentice mechanic: the first garage boy to actually attend college on day release 9.00am-9.00pm on Tuesdays. The result, after 3 years slog, being a City & Guilds Certificate.

After a while I realised that perhaps this wasn't for me and decided I would like to change direction. A few jobs followed including National Tyre Service and welding in an exhaust factory but I was drawn back to lorries and worked for B & S haulage at Tean. Here I was again 'on the spanners' but as I was approaching 21 I wanted to get on the road. I had a few trips out in the old Ford D Series 7.5 tonner but I wanted to play with the big boys!

So, I helped re-furbish a Bedford KM tipper (ex-Lymers of Tean) and took my test. The

This is a D Scragg Thorneycroft Trusty, loaded with de-gelatinised bone. The photo was taken at China and Earthenware Millers, King Street, Fenton. The man on top is driver Freddie Maybury. This picture was used by Thorneycroft in their adverts - Carl has a copy of *Commercial Motor* with it on the front cover.
Carl Johnson Collection

Taken on Cheadle car park in the early 1960s - another of of D Scragg's of Cheadle.
The one behind is Jimmy Frost's of Wolstanton. *Carl Johnson Collection*

Bedford then became my lorry and I was away on local quarry work and loving it.

As always, a change of direction saw my next driving job in 1977 at Stuart Roy & Co Ltd. This was an own account operator and here I had a Ford D Series doing mostly local work. A few years of this and I got promoted to first Foreman and then Works Manager.

One ambition I had always had was to preserve a lorry so I bought a KV ERF which was an ex-Scottish Brewers lorry. This took many years to restore but, due to the fastidious attention to detail taught to me by James Shirley (Jnr), I took it all in my stride. The only professional part of the restoration being the paint job (paint was expensive) and the services of an auto electrician for the re-wire.

In 1988 I joined the newly formed Register of ERF Vehicles Society (REVS). I was the third member but the first member that actually owned an ERF lorry. Later on I was to buy a second ERF, this time an A Series which was ex-Bowkers of Blackburn. It had a beaver tail recovery body and it was intended to take the KV to rallies on the back of this as the KV was very slow on the road and shook you to bits!

I was made Chairman of REVS at the inaugural meeting and REVS became a big part of my life. My greatest achievement was the Coming Home-Moving Home event in 2000 when ERF moved factory from Sandbach to Middlewich. Working closely with ERF

Carl in his office with his vast collection of slides. 2011.

and Bill Brookes as liaison officer I found myself involved at all levels which included meeting lots of dignitaries, even the original designer Ernest Sherratt along with Peter Foden. Of course a lot of the REVS members helped on the day and I will be forever in their debt for their support.

My time at REVS also saw the club becoming a limited company and I set up the accounting system. The old photocopied newsletter became a full colour A5 magazine and we were granted official recognition from the DVLA to advise on the retention of original registration numbers. We got the membership on a database to aid the membership secretary and we even had a licence under the Lotteries and Gaming regulations to hold raffles - the annual Christmas raffle being a very useful source of additional revenue and it helps to keep subscriptions at a sensible level.

However, all good things come to an end and due to personal circumstances I sold my lorries and resigned my position (Chief Executive Officer) at REVS in 2006. For my efforts over the years I was made a life member by the REVS directors for which I am eternally grateful.

However other aspects of my life still had me 'behind the wheel' and during holiday periods I did casual driving for Moss & Lovatt at Rushton Spencer delivering anywhere and everywhere on general haulage. I also helped local showman Paul Warwick driving his lorries but I found helping to build up the rides hard going! I certainly saw life with Paul and we went to such far flung places as the Sunderland Air Show, a nightclub at Rochester, Stamford Fair and all the regular fairs. I thoroughly enjoyed driving the Foden 6 wheeler pulling the 'Earth Shaker' Miami ride and sometimes I even had a second trailer or caravan behind; threading that little lot around took some skill. Christmas time and New Year used to see us with the fair at a local nightclub where it was an education to watch some of the antics!

One thing I have enjoyed for many years is taking photographs of lorries and I give slide shows. Normally this is easy as it's preaching to the converted, however, last year I found myself giving a presentation to the Ashbourne Rotary Club. This got me a free lunch and a seat on the top table with the president!

Giving slide shows has taken me to York and Cornwall. One of my most unusual presentations was in the pay box of Jamie Whitings Dodgems at one of the nightclub functions!

I have also written a few articles for club magazines. I'm a Committee member and organise speakers for the HCVS. I'm currently fully employed and living on my own so unfortunately I don't have the time to be as involved with my hobby as I used to. But I still enjoy reading and writing about lorries and if anyone feels they would like a slide show please contact me.

Carl with his 1963 KV ERF, ex-Scottish Brewers.
Carl Johnson Collection